# Bottoms Up!

# Bottoms Up!

Richard Ingrams & John Wells
Illustrated by George Adamson

PRIVATE EYE/ANDRÉ DEUTSCH

Published in Great Britain by Private Eye Productions Ltd,
6 Carlisle Street, London W1

© 1984 Pressdram Ltd
Illustrations by George Adamson © 1984

Reprinted 1984, 1985 (twice)

ISBN 233 97701 5

Printed by Butler & Tanner Ltd, Frome and London
Typeset by JH Graphics Ltd, Reading

6 MAY 1983

Dear Bill,

You really must forgive me for blowing my top on the phone last night, but if I haven't found out about my availability for the Algarve trip it isn't for want of trying. On sober reflection I think your best plan is to book the other ticket in the name of Smith, and then if the worst comes to the worst I'm sure Maurice P will take my place. You may not fancy two weeks sharing a Portuguese chalet, albeit with patio, with the poor old soak, but it would do him good to get away from this new home computer nonsense. I don't know if you've been down there recently, but he has somehow or other raised a loan to buy a warehouse full of obsolete word processors in Milton Keynes, and is currently working with an unemployed Jap waiter trying to decipher the assembly instructions.

It's not often, as you know, Bill, that I lose my rag with the old lady, having learned the consequences of such folly at an early stage in our ongoing matrimonial experience. Last evening, though, some moments before your reverse charge call to Downing Street, I took the opportunity to broach once again in the most tactful and diplomatic terms the question of the electoral timetable. M was doing her red boxes over supper, including Whitelaw's latest cock-eyed scheme for channelling 57 Varieties of colour TV into every chicken coop in the land – Memo: possibly an opening here for Maurice when Picatel bites the dust – and after a few preparatory coughs and a refill of the nosebag, I produced my diary, and let fly on the following lines: 'Ahem, ahem, Margaret. Excuse me for distracting you from weightier matters, but I wonder if we could have a word?' The Boss, tearing up Whitelaw's proposals: 'What is it now?' Self: 'Forward planning. It is not solely the question of my Portuguese arrangements, as you appear to think: a whole range of important engagements are hanging fire as a result of the uncertainty. Look at this. "Mr Terry Wogan on behalf of the Royal Order of Sewage Rats requests me to take the chair at a fund-raising It's a Knockout Evening in aid of mentally-handicapped Rugger Referees, on June 23rd 1983." And here's another. "The Grand

Barker of the Worshipful Company of Water Buffaloes requests the company of Mr D. Thatcher to propose the Loyal Toast at the Essoldo Ealing on June 15th. RSVP." "Mr Danny La Rue and Friends request the pleasure of Mr Denis Thatcher at a Celebrity Golf Tournament at Troon on July 1st. All proceeds to The Queen Mother's Fund for Indigent Acrobats" . . .'

Three strong cards, I think you must agree, and quite enough I would have said to force the old girl to show her hand. I laid them on the table in front of her and sat back, explaining in a firm tone that it was quite impossible to live one's life without being able to give a firm answer to these very important people. Somewhat to my chagrin, I saw that Margaret was now forking M & S lasagne into her mouth while simultaneously wielding the blue pencil on other proposals from Cabinet.

At this point, for the first time in seventeen years, my reserve gave way, and I rose to my feet, overturning a chair, and struck the table a painful blow with my fist. Was it too much to ask that my feelings should be taken into consideration? At some time in the next year, no doubt to be determined by that pompous fathead Van der Pump and a couple of oily wops from Denmark Street, I would be expected to sacrifice three weeks to traipse round the country by fast car and helicopter, crammed in with the evil-smelling little Gow and smartyboots Bertie Mount, thrown out to press the flesh of thousands of malodorous proles, a permanent grin making my face ache, an object of uproarious derision to the reptiles of Fleet Street all waiting for me to put my foot in it, listening to the same fatuous platitudes night after night, clapping like a demented monkey at the ghastly jokes of Sir Custardface, snorts snatched from my hand, digestion ruined, blistered mitts, sore feet, and all I would have to look forward to at the end of it another four years of purgatory, locked in this hell-hole, when we could be living in quiet retirement at Lamberhurst like everyone else.

I was still in full flood when I became aware that Margaret was telephoning Doctor O'Gooley on the scrambler, informing him in injured tones that I was having one of my turns, after which she left the room, locking the door behind her. The medic, I must say, could not have been more understanding (when he turned up two hours later) and told me in confidence that he often had the same sort of trouble with Mrs O'G. Boris, who is also very supportive on these occasions, produced a magnum of some unspeakably vile Cuban whisky, and we spent a pleasant enough

evening watching a smutty video confiscated by Whitelaw in one
of his lightning swoops on Huddersfield.

Arrivederci antiquo amigo mio,

Yours aye,

DENIS

Dear Bill,

Well, the whistle has finally blown, as you may have gathered from the newspapers. So much for Portugal, and I hope you will enjoy your fortnight in the sun with Maurice. Do make sure he takes his Antabuse. I know from experience the only way to do it is to actually see him swallowing them, and don't let him substitute Aspro like poor Squiffy's mother-in-law used to do towards the end. The only thing he's not allowed to have is cheese or asparagus.

They finally got the old girl over the sticks by cornering her at Chequers. M until that point, as you know, had been hopping round like a parrot telling everyone she would not be pushed about, and the nerves of the Cabinet were as much in tatters as mine. Whitelaw in particular seemed in danger of apoplexy, and poor old Hailsham who doesn't know where he is half the time anyway was obviously heading for the funny farm.

Enter at this juncture the strong men, to wit Alberto and Luigi from the advertising agency, armed with all manner of computer printouts, little graphs, market research bulletins and assorted sales guff. According to the Corsican Brothers (absolute baloney as it turned out) Worzel was on the up and up, a discernible trend with A, B and C consumers, liable to peak into Margaret's share of the market by late August. This could produce a downturn in sales figures for the month of October in image-related selling profile, spelling doom for an Autumn scenario. You remember the way those buggers at Burmah Oil used to carry on at the sales conference. What were they called – Carfax and Malpractice? I never believed a word of it, and I think they are now working for Breakfast Television. Anyway you could apparently see, according to Boris – I was upstairs at the time unpacking my weekend iron rations from Hedges and Butler – that M's eyes were clouding over with self-doubt. Here she was, her whole act as far as the plebs is concerned based on unflappability, determination to see the job through, no time for siren voices etc, how was it going to look if she was seen to be behaving like a human being, snatching at the first straw?

The meeting before lunch broke up in a mood of quiet desperation, Howe and Pym gnawing their nails down to the knuckle, both taking refuge in my little hideaway under the roof and polishing off a goodly proportion of my emergency supplies before being summoned with shrill tones to go down for their packed lunch supplied by THF in the Conference Room. Imagine their surprise, after three quarters of an hour trying to unpick the clingfoil and extract the khaki-coloured chicken leg, when the Proprietor swept in, all smiles and announced that after long and careful consideration she had decided to go on the TV and explain to the nation how imperative it was to bring an end to all this uncertainty. Pretty rich, I think you will agree, Bill, after she's spent the last two months refusing to give a straight answer to any question on the topic.

What had happened in the interim, you may ask? I will tell you. At five past one I took a call from an obviously excited Van der Pump, the South African explorer wallah who guides the nation's destinies from behind the throne. Could he speak to Mrs Thatcher at once as he had urgent information to impart. Knowing that M has such a soft spot for this oddball, I took the liberty of listening in on the extension as she came to the phone.

The old boy was plainly on a terrific high, enunciating his words with a frenzied precision. He had been up in his observatory all night, gazing into the heavens, all the wonders of the starry sky spread out before him. Margaret at this point told him to get on with it, much to my relief, as I had left my snort in the other room. He would come to the point at once, he said. A magnificent comet trailing a great banner of light across the firmament was approaching the earth at a speed of three million miles an hour and would be clearly visible with the naked eye in a night or two's time, weather conditions permitting. 'What does it portend, Prime Minister, you may ask.' 'I do ask,' came the somewhat impatient rejoinder. 'Victory,' breathed the sage in a voice fraught with strange significance. 'For those born under the sign of Libra this is an important week with regard to a vital business decision. Colleagues' advice should be heeded. With new heavenly movements affecting your cusp, now is the time to end uncertainties and tell your nearest and dearest of your decision. Your love-partner will be relieved, as he or she will be able to make plans at last in the realm of leisure activities.' 'You can say that again,' I unwisely expostulated, only bringing down on myself a torrent of abuse from M for eavesdropping and a command to hang up at once.

What worries me, Bill, at least the way things look at the moment, is that my worst fears about another four years of misery cooped up in purdah in a back room at Downing Street seem all too justified. With a two hundred seat majority, can you imagine what she'll be like? You don't think you could have a word with your Grand Master to pass the word round among the brethren that a vote for Labour might be in order, just to balance things out a bit? Otherwise I can see myself following old Hailsham into the Priory.

Pip, pip,

DENIS

3 JUNE 1983

Dear Bill,

Only another week to go before polling day, thank God. My hand is already calloused and misshapen from pressing the proletarian flesh and Dr O'Gooley had to pop in the other day to give me an anti-lockjaw injection after three weeks of solid grinning. Then last night I woke up shouting 'Hear Hear' in response to Margaret's snores, which will give you some idea of how far things have gone. I wish I could be more sanguine about the future, but it does now look as if I must face the prospect of another four to five years incarcerated in Colditz SW1. Picturing you and Maurice hot-footing it over the sprinklered sward of the Algarve en route to Mrs Flack's beachside Smugglers' Bar only serves to twist the knife in the wound.

Personally, I blame Worzel for all this. The poor old fool's always been hopelessly out of his depth in that tank of piranha fish and you can tell from the expression on his face that they've got to him. Immediately the charge was sounded half of his Red Lancers turned on one another, pigsticking away as if there was no tomorrow, while Uncle Jim Callaghan sounded his own private tally-ho shortly afterwards to distract the remaining ditherers from the battle. All that remains now is for that old twister Wilson to crawl out from under his stone and inject his lethal venom into Worzel's unprotected hinder parts, and they'll have to blow up for a walk-over. When you've seen our lot at close quarters, particularly that fat ass Howe, little Bertie Mount beavering away with his Roget's Thesaurus trying to think of something new for M to say, Sir Custardface on call with his dressing gown and gag book, and Gow fartarsing about the place, you'd think anyone with a grain of intelligence could blow them off the map.

As it is the projected majority gets bigger every day with all the grave implications that entails for the Boss's mental equilibrium. It was plainly this thought that occurred to Brother Pym when he blurted out on TV that the last thing he wanted was a landslide. Of course he was immediately summoned round to explain himself to the Supreme Commander. It is quite pathetic to see these men, Bill, crumbling before one's eyes under the impact of the deadly gamma rays. Afterwards little Pym got very tight with some reptile and told him he wasn't budging from the FO whatever happened, but I think if truth be told he's already reconciled to the heave-ho come the July purge and has been seen scanning the Occupations Vacant column in the Farmers' Weekly.

Old Oystereyes is in much the same boat, and has, alas, been looking pretty deep into the glass in a forlorn attempt to muffle the pain. Fatty Prior, poor old sod, remains in exile in the Bogs, and if he is waiting for a recall I fear he may wait in vain. The Monk is keeping very quiet with the help of a big bottle of green pills which he stores in his briefcase and shovels into his mouth every ten minutes in generous quantities.

The only good thing to come out of the whole farrago so far is that the fat cat Jenkins has quite clearly thrown in the towel as far as a career in politics is concerned. I always told Maurice they made a great mistake when they put him in charge, and I bet little Steel is absolutely livid: being seen about with the old fool must have cost him ninety-nine per cent of any seats he hoped to win. Apropos, I'd be very interested to know if the voters of Sevenoaks have realised that their Social Democratic candidate, Maurice Picarda Esq, has hopped it to Portugal, taking with him, I gather, a large proportion of the campaign funds. How much will he give me, I wonder, for not ringing up the Sevenoaks Chronicle and spilling the beans? I gather quite a lot of the SDP folk have deemed it prudent to go abroad till the whole thing blows over.

I hope you can read this, despite the odd typing error, but I am writing in the back of the Saatchimobile haring up the M1 to some derelict marginal in the North West. The Corsican Brothers are sucking spaghetti through their moustaches at the other end of the table, and friend Gow is on his back with a screwdriver trying to mend Margaret's Hopalong Teleprompter which went on the blink at the last whistlestop and caused a good deal of Proprietorial gnashing of teeth. Little Cecil Parkinson, unruffled as ever, is chatting up the Boss with a look of doglike devotion in his eyes, and giving me a frosty glare every time I have recourse to my flask, as much as to say how could a man married to this paragon possibly be in need of any other solace or stimulant. Little does he know.

Roll on death,

DENIS

17 JUNE 1983

Dear Bill,

Well, that's it! What a ballcrushing disaster! In all my wildest nightmares I never visualised it being quite as bad as this. Another five years of guaranteed hard labour as a tailor's dummy being wheeled on to grin to order every time the Boss plays host to the likes of Hopalong, Big Chief Coon or Ahmed ben Wog. The trouble is I've seen them already, and if the novelty was ever in danger of wearing on, it's certainly worn off now.

One of the reptiles the other day, while we were being shuttled to and from A to Z, told me en passant that Jackie Kennedy negotiated a pretty fat retainer for staying on in the supporting role. I did think of approaching Top Management with a strike ultimatum, proposing a minimum three months in six off the leash, all expenses paid and a company flat in sunny parts, but the Boss is still in overdrive after Friday morning's results and shows no sign of shifting into a lower gear.

Boris, to whom I confided my post-election thoughts of self-destruction, said I should look at it more positively. It was tempting to sit on the sidelines, large tincture in hand and carp at the passing show, encouraging a mood of Scandinavian despondency. Far better to plunge in while I was still active, and play a more decisive role in the affairs of state.

It may have been his silver tongue or possibly the effects of a second crate of his widowed mother's plum vodka, but the prospect began to seem a great deal rosier. I mean quite honestly, Bill, with all the power in the country concentrated in the hands of wets and waverers like Norman Tebbit, what hope of any real upturn? Now, surely – this is what Boris said – we have the chance to crack down on troublemakers, pack up the railways and other drains on the motorist's pocket, remove tax from heavy spirits, hand over the NHS to BUPA, introduce imprisonment without trial for all shop stewards, bring back the black cap and other long overdue middle-of-the-road reforms. Rather late at night admittedly, I noted down a few of these ideas on a paper doily and stuffed them under the door of little Bertie Mount, Margaret's one-man think-tank. And as you will see from the reshuffled Cabinet, some of my notions are beginning to trickle

through, and I have reason to hope that as time goes on I shall be able to get my hand more firmly on the tiller.

I still maintain we could have been out from under it altogether and sipping the pina colada chez Mother Flack beneath the thatched parasols of the Algarve, had it not been for that frightful old stumblebum Worzel Gummidge and his entourage of hopeless clowns and kamikaze wallahs. By the end of it even Koalafeatures lost his marbles altogether, and was throwing away votes like confetti. I've no idea who they'll find now to preside over the salvage operations on the Red Titanic, but I understand the leading contenders are that red-haired Welsh windbag called Pillock and some wheezing fat cat from Birmingham who contributes would-be humorous pieces to Punch. I can't understand why they don't just pack their bags and bugger off back to Moscow.

There were one or two happier moments on Thursday night I must confess, eg Benn walking the plank, ditto Benn junior. Margaret only really showed her teeth when the woman with the messy hair came unstuck at Crosby. I was also personally very gratified to see a frightful little greaser called Sprat or Sproat bite the dust: he's tried to oil up to me at the Club once or twice affecting an interest in golf, but it was perfectly clear he didn't know a mashie from a swizzle stick. Maurice, I see, managed to scrape in just ahead of the National Front despite his absence on foreign soil, and incidentally thank you very much for your postcard: I couldn't decipher the old boy's remarks but I liked the photograph of the lady holding her hat on and the bloke lurking in the shallows with a snorkel.

The musical chairs in the Cabinet began on Friday morning. Poor little Pym trotted round to the Headmistress's study soon after breakfast and was told it was to be six of the best and immediate expulsion for dumb insolence. Old Oystereyes blubbed a lot, put an arm round the boy's shoulders and pleaded for his chum in a very pathetic way. The Boss however remained unmoved, giving them both the gamma ray treatment. Pym got five minutes to pack his tuck box before being driven to the station. Oystereyes himself has been kicked upstairs and given an Hereditary Peerage. I said to Margaret what was the point of this as his only male relative is a bus driver living in Scunthorpe but she only gave me a frosty smile. I suppose she must be allowed her little joke. Talking of jokes old Hailsham will not after all be heading for the funny farm, but is to be kept on for the sake of the tourists. Lawson and Brittan, those two frightful little creeps who Margaret has taken such a shine to, have both been promoted for services to the brown-tongue industry. But more of them later.

So there we are. I don't know whether you've ever made a will, but for some reason or other the thought had never occurred to me until last Friday morning. Furniss has a printed form you can fill in, costing 30p, and I said I didn't mind what he put as long as Mark didn't get his grubby little hands on any of it and there was some provision for scattering my ashes in the bunker opposite the Club House at Worplesdon. Furniss said there wasn't a space on the form for that kind of thing. Could I leave it to you to make the arrangements when the Reaper comes to call? On a more serious note, M owes me a favour if nothing more after my loyal laughter and rigid lips-sealed policy vis-a-vis the reptiles. What price three weeks in Gib before the FO wooftahs hand it back on a plate to King Coca Cola?

Adios,

DENIS

10 Downing Street
Whitehall

15 JULY 1983

Dear Bill,

As you see, I'm back from my little hol, not too much the worse for wear and already wishing I wasn't. Whoever it was, though, who told you that there was some lovely golf to be had in Malta is talking through his arse. Either that or he meant somewhere else. The place is a rock-strewn dump inhabited by swarthy degenerates, Spanish waiters and sex fiends on the run from Interpol. I tried to look up Purvis, who as you remember retired there with his pile of chips in the early sixties, but according to the woman living in the house, he was driven out some years ago by this little commie Dom Molotoff, who now runs the place. You probably remember his daughter threw a sack of donkey droppings into the House of Commons some while ago; probably the only decent thing any member of that family has ever done.

I got back to find Margaret in no way improved, and chuckling over the news that poor little Steel can't stand the pace and is sodding off back to bonnie Scotland to collapse in a deep arm-chair for the summer. The Boss was very amused when one of her brown-tongue brigade on the back benches pointed out that since June 9th Worzel and Woy had both jacked it in, Kinnock had lost the power of speech, and now little Steel has had a nervous breakdown. Alas, there is no sign of anything like that happening to the Boss.

One unhappy consequence of the recent musical chairs is that old Howe alias Mr Mogadon, but a very quiet neighbour given to padding cautiously about in his brothel creepers accompanied by a mildly talkative wife droning away in the background, has now been replaced next door at Number Eleven by Mr Nicely Nicely Lawson. According to Frognall, who lost a packet on John Bloom with the washing machines, Lawson used to be some kind of share spiv for the Sunday Telegraph, offering the punters likely tips on the City Page. I gather his wife ran off with some randy egg-head from Oxford, for which I must say I can't entirely blame her. He is now encumbered with a librarian woman and presides, if that is the word for it, over an unruly family, definitely the non-nuclear variety, hence the thump of pop

records mingled with the squalling of babies hourly audible through the wall.

I can't quite fathom what the Boss sees in him myself. We had them both round for a snort a couple of evenings ago, a social occasion that could, I must say, have gone more smoothly. Mrs L rather a nervous little body, sat primly to attention, listening to Margaret banging on about the future of the Falklands, nodding tentatively every ten minutes as if afraid she was going to bite her, and Lawson himself got very man to man with Yours Truly, shovelling salted peanuts into his mouth and saying 'I think Denis, that you and I have at least one recreation in common, and it isn't golf, eh?' I couldn't see what he was driving at. Then he winked, nodded at the bottle, and held out his glass, which I refilled, still very mystified. It was only after he'd gone, that Boris suggested he was probably suggesting I was a piss-artist. Cheeky little bugger.

Anyway, he seems to have got off to a good start, announcing without so much as turning a hair that we weren't on the road to recovery after all, but that on the contrary we were up the familiar creek fabled in song and story in a barbed wire canoe sans paddle, and that the axe must therefore fall on all the various sacred cows paraded out at the election. I gather Ginger Jesus, which is what old Hailsham calls Heseltine, is absolutely livid as only the day before he'd announced the biggest-ever shopping spree for the Brasshats, including a new Tumbledown International Airport for the Falklands, devised by some bright spark as an inducement to the Sheepshaggers to pack their bags and whiz away to healthier climes. Personally I don't think they're clever enough for that, and when they're all pulling down a million and a half per man, woman and sheep from the British taxpayer one can't really wonder at their staying.

The Boss's other bright-eyed boy, called Brittan, is a smarmy lawyer from somewhere in Transylvania, who has taken over from poor old Whitelaw; Oystereyes having finally been wheeled away to the red-leather Geriatrics' Ward just across from the H of C. I thought he'd made a promising debut, with plans to bring back the rope, something in my view they should have done years ago. All the wets like Whitelaw and Runcie go on about it being barbaric and so forth, but certainly in the Club people are queueing up to pull the lever, and from a humanitarian point of view I'm told that most killers would prefer to take the short sharp shock any time rather than wither away in jug being visited by that awful old RC chap in the dirty raincoat.

They've now got round to a vote on it, but when it comes to the crunch and Dracula Brittan gets up and shows his fangs you can bet your bottom dollar it'll be the usual woolly Guardian rubbish that will win the day. I can't help suspecting that the old girl's heart isn't really in it. Whatever she says it hasn't got mass consumer appeal like the Falklands.

What of my further holiday plans, you ask? The widow Glover is making coaxing noises from Schloss Bangelstein with a new dentist thrown in to re-do M's teeth after last year's disaster: Lord Pucefeatures has sent smoke signals urging attendance on the Isle of Muck, and the Reagans have offered us a self-catering ranch somewhere in Wyoming. But the Boss is still dithering, and since the news about Steel I think it's quite possible she'll put her head down and work through, just to rub his nose in it. This would suit me fine as the scenarios mentioned above have never exactly set me afire. I enclose a package suggestion from a bucket shop Maurice has something to do with in Balham: I know Iceland doesn't sound all that appetising, but there's no night at all there in summer, so it could mean they never close. I have asked Boris to research the possibilities.

Yours incoherently,

DENIS

10 Downing Street
Whitehall

29 JULY 1983

Dear Bill,

How are you coping with the heat down in Kent? Up here it's quite intolerable, yobbos loafing about in their underpants, every kind of tourist riff-raff loitering outside the door with Instamatics waiting for something to happen. When I turned the sprinkler on the other afternoon little Bertie Mount came scurrying out with a message from the Boss to turn it off immediately or Red Ken would be over the wall before you could say knife. I can't understand where all the water goes to, can you? Two months ago it was bucketing down like Niagara Falls and it can't have just disappeared.

I've spent most of the heat wave in a pair of Lillywhites shorts sprawled in a canvas chair in front of the TV watching Birkdale, my silver locks ruffled by a fan borrowed from the Cabinet office. Boris doesn't like the heat at all, and has come out in a rash on the soles of his feet which makes him very grumpy. By the by, your Golfer's Portable Oasis from that mail order shop in Texas has come in jolly handy during the drought. I put the Pimm's in first thing in the morning, fill the ice compartment as per instructions, and it's still delightfully chilled when I drain the last snort before toddling down to the Club for a quick one at noon.

You saw they cocked up the hanging business as I confidently predicted? Personally I blame little Dracula Teeth Brittan for the fiasco. Here were the new boys, no idea of the form, all perfectly prepared in their rather numskulled way to kill for Margaret on command, and where was the clarion voice to tell them where

their duty lay? Instead, up pops the Hammer film hero, poised as one might think to outline the advantages of slow strangulation, all the colourful nostalgia of the black cap, the last hearty breakfast, the walk to the scaffold, the creak of the lever, the light in the executioner's eye as the trap falls open and a ragged cheer goes up from the chaplain and bystanders. Not so. The oily Transylvanian hums and hahs, vaguely trying to catch Margaret's eye to see what it is she really wants, and eventually sits down leaving the new recruits under the impression that what would really bring a smile to the Proprietor's lips is a vote against the rope. Which may in fact have been the case, if you ask me, but I have long since stopped expecting any kind of logic from the Boss.

Next on the agenda at Halitosis Hall is the question of how much the useless prats thought they ought to award themselves in the way of a pay hike. They were already taking home what you or I would call a bloody good screw for unskilled middle management, not to mention 'expenses', ie secretaries, chauffeurs, cut price snorts in the basement, and on top of that, as you know most of them are moonlighting to the tune of several thou a year sitting on boards, running fish and chip shops and so forth in their spare time. The Boss made a very generous offer of four per cent, upon which a howl of outrage went up from the assembled deadbeats and idlers, all of whom had got their sights set on the prospect of thirty rising to sixty over the next three years. As it is they're all about to bugger off for two months' fully paid holiday. The latest proposal put forward by that smarmy greaser Edward du Cann acting as ACAS is that they should be kept in line with civil servants with index-linked perks and a full pension after six months in the job. I understand now why Maurice was so keen to do his bit for the community.

Did you read about little Pillock's amazing prang on the M4? It said on the news he was stone cold sober, and I suppose one should rule out foul play with the monkey wrench by the Hattersley Dirty Tricks Brigade, which makes it all very mysterious. It crossed Boris's mind that the whole thing was a shrewd publicity stunt, which would explain why the Newbury News photographer was standing by on the hard shoulder when he landed. Can this be right? No matter. The feeling in this neck of the woods is that Pillock has got the job in the bag and a damn good thing too as he is just another version of Worzel only Welsh and younger and not so intelligent.

Still no news from the oracle about the hols. From the various runic inscriptions in Margaret's Dataday it could be Balmoral, or, horror of horrors, the Isle of Muck. Maurice Picarda has been ringing very persistently. He and some of his Sevenoaks rotarians have formed a consortium to buy the Southern Railway, or at least the profitable bits, when it comes on the market. I said I didn't think there were any profitable bits, but I would ask Lawson the next time we have our usual disagreement about parking spaces. I think it's beginning to dawn on the Boss that she's made a bit of a boo-boo letting poor old Howe off the leash and bringing in this new wide boy with his long eyelashes and lah-di-dah ways. Apparently he used to tip shares on the Sunday Telegraph. Did I tell you that before? I find I am constantly repeating myself these days. I find that I am constantly repeating myself these days. I shall be forgetting my own name next.

Yours through the haze,

BORIS

Dear Bill,

As you see from the above, the Widow Glover won on points over Lord Pucefeatures and the Reagan Ranch House, and thus it is that I find myself typing this on the deceased's electric Remington to the sound of cuckoo clocks and distant alpenhorns. The routine chez Mere Glover is if anything more grisly than last year. I put this down largely to the bulky presence of the Widow's Swiss friend, Herr Doktor Bosendorfer, an elderly bearded shrink and close friend of Van der Pump. In addition to his other quirks, ie deafness, inability to speak comprehensible English, unsteadiness on the pins etc, the Doctor is a teetotaller, who tells me he regards my own way of life as pathologically unstable.

In order to escape the presence of this heavy-footed weirdo on whose company circumstances here inevitably thrust me for a good deal of the time, I have been forced to invent a business contact in Bern called Herr Zwingli, with whom I arrange regular assignments, working lunches, and even occasionally small dinner parties. At whatever hour of the day or night I return Doctor Bosendorfer is always there waiting to interrogate me about our business, other guests, the menu and so forth, nodding at my answers and saying 'Ya, ya, ya. Please go on,' like some mad gestapo chief questioning a recently recaptured squadron leader from Colditz.

You must have read all about M's eye operation. She has asked me to thank you and Daphne for the white stick. She's knocking off fifty thank you letters every morning before breakfast, so I've no doubt she'll get round to you eventually and you'll receive your signed photograph to put on top of the piano with all the other ones.

The trouble with the Boss of course is that she hates to admit to any form of weakness, and has been known to hit Cabinet ministers who stand up and offer her a seat. I spotted that there was something agley even before the Election, when she started going cross-eyed trying to read the Hopalong Teleprompter Screen, and advised her to have a word with Doctor O'Gooley. I was told not to be ridiculous, he was a hopeless drunk who couldn't read a thermometer even if someone held his hand to stop it trembling, and anyway he was National Health and wouldn't be able to see her for months.

When things worsened and tempers became frayed as I inevitably knew they would, some very sharp little number was summoned round from Harley Street who I think must have been a friend of Lawson's. To begin with they tried to keep the whole thing secret and Dr Kildare, or whatever his name was, offered it as his opinion that it could all be sorted out in a couple of shakes after closing hours with a blast of his death ray machine. We were all accordingly swept round under cover of darkness to some sort of Star Wars set-up at fifty guineas a minute. Of course it turned out that Margaret fused the machine and the whole thing was a complete bloody waste of time, at which point I suggested trying O'Gooley again. I might as well have been talking to the wall, and probably was by that time. Second Doctor wheeled in, a very smooth little BUPA chap called Pankhurst or some such name, his line being a simple little op, he does fifty of them a week, nice quiet clinic in the backstreets of Windsor, very tasty food, same butcher as the Castle, far from prying eyes of Fleet Street, he'd have her in and out in a couple of days and no one would be the wiser.

You probably saw our arrival on television, police having to hold back photographers. Someone below stairs had let the cat out of the bag and from then on it was sheer hell, yours truly being picked on by the powers that be to give the nightly bulletins before the cameras and respond to the barrage of idiot questions from the foul-breathed yobbos. 'Is she working under the anaesthetic?' 'What's the hospitality like then, Denis?' and similar impertinencies. Even so I think I managed to keep my end up and scored a moderate hit with the little man at Saatchis who does the TV advertising.

What had her really hopping mad, even under the anaesthetic, was the allegation that no proper chain of command had been established to deal with any emergency in her absence. It transpired that in the event of war breaking out while she was in the operating theatre, the man in charge was poor old Willie Whitelaw, or Lord Lakedistrict as he is now. I said the chances were he'd be out on the links anyway, if he wasn't half cut, or both, and even then I very much doubted if he'd be able to find the button with both hands. Apropos, I may have said this before, but it seems a damn silly idea giving hereditary honours to two old buffers with no male heir. What's the point? If that's the qualification, why not give one to our seafaring friend Ted Heath, or Stevarse for that matter? I made the mistake of suggesting this in a rash moment the other night when Margaret and the Widow Glover were watching the stockmarket prices live from Zurich, and it went down like a lead balloon, especially when Doctor Bosendorfer woke up and asked to have it explained.

Tomorrow we climb the Matterhorn in the funicular for a picnic with an aunt and former patient of the Doctor who lives in a chalet and has a collection of English glass paperweights. I fear Herr Zwingli may have to send one of his telegrams summoning me to crisis talks in the Etoile Keller. Auf Wiedersehen, mein alter freund.

Bergmanns Heil!

DENIS

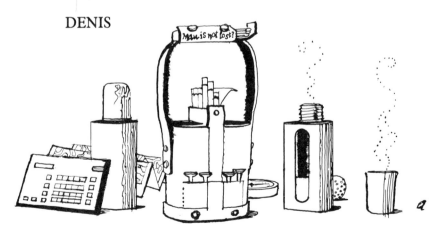

Dear Bill,

Many many thanks for your aerogramme, which was brought up from the village yesterday by Herr Bosendorfer who had been down to have his beard trimmed. Any little contact with the outside world here is like a puff of smoke on the horizon to a man marooned on a desert island, and I was very moved. The Telegraph arrives at the station kiosk three days late, which makes pretty good nonsense of the weather forecast and rather takes the thrill out of the crossword.

I suppose you're still basking in the heat wave in easy strolling distance of the Merry Leper, with Daphne safely packed off to her American friends in Portugal. You lucky bugger. You ask, apropos, whether there is a news blackout on our activities. The fact is that it is so boring here that even the Telegraph stringer, a little man in leather shorts called Ackroyd, went away in despair after two fruitless days lurking in the shrubbery with his telephoto lens. What the hell did he expect? At half past nine old Bosendorfer toddles down to the summerhouse with a leather bag full of case histories to mull over, the Boss meanwhile, having been at her papers since six, sits in the tower dialling away on the telephone to bring this minister or that sloshing out of swimming pools from Tenerife to Dover to give an account of their daily doings. Your old friend, having discreetly avoided the Widow, now face down on the massage couch being slapped by elderly karate expert Rosa Klebb, sets off on his constitutional via the back gate and down to the village to the Kaffeehaus Wandervogel. There, having purchased the aforementioned out-of-date copy of the Daily Telegraph from Herr Blasius the newsagent, he spends the next two hours wrestling with the crossword with a litre bottle of some colourless but potent sticky at his elbow to stimulate the grey tissues.

I thought, thanks to an alpine hat and dark glasses, that I had managed to remain incognito, until the other day the Coffee House keeper, Herr Davis, brought his own foaming stein of beer, and placing his considerable bulk directly opposite me asked whether I would settle a bet he was having with his dentist. Was I not Herr Thatcher, staying up the mountain with the

Widow? I thought for a moment of doing my halfwit act – never too difficult at that time of the morning – but in the end I owned up. There followed a riveting half hour listening to an encomium of the Boss's achievements, her superb skills as a war commander, gallant defence of firm currency, admirably truculent attitude to the Russian Bear. Since then I have had to lend an ear every morning to similar confidences, and today the dentist friend, one Herr Weidenfeld, a small excitable man with protuberant eyes, was presented, and put a number of questions about Margaret's new teeth and how much each had cost, which I was quite unable to answer. Tomorrow Frau Dr Dentist Weidenfeld and their eight children are to join us at our table for coffee and Black Forest gateau with cream.

Lunch at the Schloss is taken in silence, punctuated only by the occasional sharp explosion of the Widow's crispbread slimmers' biscuits and the soft tread of white-coated menials replenishing Herr Bosendorfer's glass with mineral water. At five to two I fold my napkin and am allowed to retire to my room to finish the crossword and try to think up excuses for cutting the afternoon excursion in Herr Hanfstaengel's limo. The fictitious Herr Zwingli of Bern, a mysterious business contact who constantly requires my eagle eye to sort out some little item of double-entry book keeping at the Etoile Keller, has been of invaluable assistance, and I have managed so far to miss the Matterhorn, an exhibition of Gruyere cheese making, a glockenspiel concert, a visit to a Calvin's birthplace, and hot chocolate with a retired Canadian stockbroker who once had control of the Widow's considerable investments.

Maurice P however having entrusted me with a triangular brown-paper parcel to deposit in Lichtenstein, I agreed to join the official party for a trip to Vaduz, capital city of the pocket-handkerchief-sized principality, the only country on earth where the Royal Family outnumbers the rest of the population by two to one. The Prince, who walked down to the border to meet us, seemed a nice enough cove in plus fours and a fairisle pullover, and said he'd heard all about me from his close friend the D of E, a fellow preserver of World Wildlife, and would I like to stay for a boar shoot the following day? If not perhaps I might prefer to see his collection of postage stamps? Foreseeing another morass of tedium, and noting that Margaret and the Widow were scheduled for a conducted tour of the conservatory with the Archduchess Brunhilde, I asked His Serene Highness if it was all the same to him if I popped down to the town to buy a pair of shoes. Imagine my horror, as I slipped past the sentries at the gate, to see Herr Bosendorfer, who had been eyeing me strangely and no doubt suspects me of every kind of secret vice, tottering along in my wake. I gave him the slip easily enough by taking a short cut through the cathedral, and had no trouble in finding the International Head Office of the Pan-African Bank, located with fifty other undertakings in the front room of a small terraced house. As I rounded the corner however the sight of two burly agents of the law lurking at the threshold fingering their riot sticks, and a third sitting in a car opposite talking to base on his walkie talkie made me think twice about entering. Sure enough at that very instant a man carrying an identical parcel to mine arrived at the door, was snatched roughly off his feet, and thrown into the boot of the car.

Back at the Palace for tea with various old fossils in coronets and eight rows of pearls who had been wheeled out for our inspection, all totally gaga, I heard Bosendorfer, mopping his brow and with his suit clinging to him from his exertions, observing to the Boss that he had no idea I was so deeply religious –'A whole hour in the cathedral! Tell me about his mother.' The Boss gave us both a pretty beady look and was fortunately swept away to see His Highness's showjumping trophies.

Roll on Balmoral!

Yours in extremis,

DENIS

**BALMORAL CASTLE**          **TEL: BALLATER 3**
**ABERDEENSHIRE**       **STATION: BALLATER**
**SCOTLAND**

9 SEPTEMBER 1983

Dear Bill,

Out of the frying pan into the fire. After a brief stopover in London – the only things on the mat being an obscene postcard from the Major (currently living it up in Minorca with Barmy Hodgkiss and his nightclub floozie, the one who was married to a Labour peer and went to tap-dancing lessons in the evening before she broke her leg), two bills from Lillywhites and a circular from some crooked stockbroker recommended by Maurice – we were immediately shot off by the Saatchis on a Scottish whistle-stop of the economic disaster areas. We steered well clear of the Clyde, notorious as a breeding ground for every kind of Bolshevik agitator, and called in on two bicycle factories and the only computer works in Auchtermuchty where they'd still got the roof on and the machines working. The Boss did her best to pour the old flannel over the latest unemployment figures by pointing out to the tame reptiles present that Interscan Software Auchtermuchty (formerly Hire-a-Bike of Auchtermuchty PLC) were at the very forefront of British technological know-how, and that the seventeen new jobs created were a first step in the long haul back to full employment. We were then entertained to warmed up haggis sandwiches and a cup of instant Macpacket Dried Scotch Broth by the manager, Mr Yamaha, who looked a bit glazed when Margaret told him she saw herself as Mr Churchill and then rather put his foot in it, when he had finally hauled in the message, by making the V sign and offering her a huge Burma cheroot.

What news from Castle o'Doom? Well, not since the Isle of Muck have I undergone such humiliations. At least at Schloss Bangelstein one was left in peace and treated as a private patient.

This lot here subscribe to the Gordonstoun Bugger Them About school of thought. Half past five yesterday morning, thump thump thump on the bedroom door – M already knee deep in international dispatches – and a mountainous Scot with a thick red beard and a kilt strides into the room, depositing a plate of concrete-like porridge on the bedside table, tearing the clothes off the bed, announcing that he has run me a cold bath and that the shooting party will be leaving in three minutes. Then there ensues a twenty-five mile drive in an ancient landrover, most of it over trackless rocks and heather, the porridge refusing to lie low despite its immense weight, three princelings of the Blood Royal singing lavatory songs at the tops of their voices and the Duke with a foot hard down on the accelerator shouting abuse at the sheep which scatter before our bouncing wheels.

Finally we ground to a halt at the head of a dark glen where a knot of purple-faced piss-artists in plus fours and green wellingtons bowed and scraped and dutifully laughed at the D of E's early morning obscenities. A bottle of whisky was passed from hand to hand but when it came to my turn the Duke snatched it from my grasp and said No no, he'd promised Margaret there would be nothing for me before lunch and then it'd be a can of shandy if I was damn lucky. (Ha, ha, ha, from the puce-featured contingent.)

After a good three hours' slog across the moor by which time my Lillywhites so-called waterproof golfing shoes were asquelch with brown water and my trousers sodden to the knees, we arrived at the butts. Amid more laughter and a further rotation of the hard stuff the Duke said that we should now draw straws for Butt Number Thirteen and Mr MacLevin. I drew last and needless to say got the short straw. More guffaws and MacLevin was brought up, also apparently in on the joke. I can never tell those two Princes apart, but the one who was in the Falklands show and mucks about with the American tarterino offered to point the way to my position, a distant speck of rock on the shoulder of a great hill where a little red flag could be discerned through binoculars fluttering on the skyline.

Come noon we were in situ. MacLevin, a former sergeant major in one of the Highland Regiments, was not a man clearly I could look to for any sympathy. He loaded my gun, thrust it into my hands, and told me I'd be lucky if I saw much game as it had been a hot summer and the heather was as dry as tinder. There was, he said, 'nae monny a groose tae tak a pottie at.' The occasional rare bang from down in the valley confirmed this view. After about an hour of further misery I at last, like that chap in the poem when the creepy things come on board and they've all got the DTs, descried a welcome shape flapping towards us at zero feet, and was raising my firing piece to prang it, when a swarthy hand grasped me by the back of the neck and hurled me to the ground. 'Dinna shoot, ye mad fule,' Mr MacLevin cried, 'can ye no tell a seagull when ye see one? His Royal Highness would hae yer breeks for garters for gunning doon the wild life!' Thinking it pointless to enter into a debate as to why the grouse should bite the dust and the seabird escape unharmed, I lit a cigarette and decided to wait for lunch.

Moments later we were engulfed in smoke, and despite MacLevin removing his kilt and attempting to beat out the burning heather the fire spread very rapidly over a sizeable area of Aberdeenshire and a pall of black smoke still hangs on the horizon as I write. Yours truly inevitably blamed for the whole episode, non grata with HM the Queen, Boss furious, officially placed on jankers by D of E, told to report to his room five times a day in different kit for an earful about the threat to vole and grasshopper, invitation from Royal and Ancient to toddle round with their pro and Lord Lakedistrict (Oystereyes as was) cancelled 'owing to lack of transport'.

Fortunately the Boss has been on a high ever since the Russkies bagged the Boeing, it being clear proof that she and Hopalong are right about the Bear. She did have the Button sent up here just in case, but I think Boris persuaded her to let him take it to bits for servicing so no harm done.

Any chance of an extended lunch at the RAC on the 20th?

Greetings frae bonnie Deeside,

DENIS

Dear Bill,

You ask me in yours of the 11th inst about this little prat with the glasses who has taken over Parkinson's job, J. Selwyn Bummer as he is known round the office. I can tell you very little about him, except that no one can understand why he has been singled out for the distinction. Boris tells me he's a Bible thumper who prints tracts of an improving nature for distribution at bus stops, and that he's got it in for the likes of you and me as limbs of Beelzebub with our miscellaneous weaknesses of the flesh. I have occasionally seen him having a giggle with Runcie at his ghastly sherry parties and he's certainly a prime candidate for the OBT (Order of the Brown Tongue), particularly where Margaret is concerned. Beyond that I'm afraid I can enlighten you no further. We shall have to wait for the Rocky Horror Show at Blackpool, where Mr Bummer will be called upon to wield the gavel and try to keep the NF contingent in order before marking his card.

Strictly entre nous, Bummer's promotion, coming in the wake of such arch creamers as Lawson and Brittan, has been interpreted by one or two sage heads here as a sign that the old girl is finally cracking up. Would that she were and we could hot foot it away to Dunleadin, Lamberhurst, Kent! Unfortunately the Opposition refuses to play along with this scenario, and until the emergence of any serious contender from Smellysocks House, the SDP mob or the Libs, she's clearly going to cling on, whatever her state of health. The reptiles did their best last week to boost the smarmy-haired little houseman Owen but as I may have said before the only decent thing he ever did was to try and break the neck of that Trot who threw a tomato at him. And as far as new SDP ideas are concerned they've obviously all been copied out of the manifesto Bertie Mount did for our people. As for Steel, the chap is clearly ripe for Picarda's open-plan funny farm. I blame *her* quite frankly. She looks like the kind of woman who stands behind the door with a rolling pin waiting for the poor little sod to totter in from an all-night sitting to crack him one over the nut. If *he* jacks it in God knows who they'll dredge up.

It's early days yet for ginger Pillock, but as hammer of the Trots I wouldn't give him the chances of a snowball in hell.

Talking of the Bolshies, did you by any chance see that extraordinary thing on the TV news of Scargill genuflecting in front of old Mr MacGregor, Margaret's all-purpose geriatric American whizz-kid? According to Boris, word came through from Andropov to the effect that he'd rather overdone it on the pro-Soviet line condemning Solidarnosc or whatever they're called and so forth, and a message had been left in the hollowed out tree telling him not to make it so obvious in future who was paying his salary. Don't breathe this around as obviously the last thing I want is Scargill's lawyers hammering on the door at Number Ten. All meant in jest and so forth and no substance to these allegations whatsoever.

Searching for allies or even civilised drinking companions in the Proprietor's new Cabinet is a pretty hopeless task, especially now poor old Oystereyes has been moved to the bed nearest the door. It may admittedly be lack of any reasonable alternative, but I could eventually come round to Heseltine. My reason for saying this is that listening to Boris's tapes of last week's Cabinet I was delighted to hear Tarzan laying into Fatty Lawson and his cheap

cuts in no uncertain terms and also being very sound on the need for dumping the Sheepshaggers once and for all. Lawson came on very pompous and started on a lot of guff about M3 and the Snake, an old gambit that Howe always used to resort to when I got him in a corner and asked him about my deposit account. But I formed the impression that Tarzan's got him marked down for his hate book. Say what you like about Heseltine, at least he was working hard and making his own way in the world like you and me when Lawson was gobbling down the canapes and pocketing the cigars as a reptile pushing dubious shares in the Sunday Telegraph. Including I may say those of the rascal Bloom, that funny little geezer with the beard and the washing machines. You remember the Major's first wife was in deep shock for three weeks after hers exploded and the Major himself came a very nasty cropper with the equities.

Now, if you please, Lawson is toddling round slamming our fingers in the till on off-shore funds and tax concessions to the big oil boys. By all means nail the pen pushers of Whitehall down to 0.003 recurring on pay increases over the next twenty-five years, but Furniss at the NatWest was saying to me only this morning over a few scoops of cooking sherry, it used to be the rule with our mob that you had people like Lawson on the inside pissing out, not the other way about.

Any chance of a day out at Wentworth, which I see is looming up yet again? If you get the limo I'll do the booze at Attwoods.

Yrs in haste,

DENIS

# 10 Downing Street
# Whitehall

7 OCTOBER 1983

Dear Bill,

Did you ever read about the man who was buried in a coffin for six months with only a tube connecting him to the outside world for some damnfool scientific experiment in France or somewhere? Well, after my five-continents-in-four-days tour with Margaret I know exactly what he felt like when they brought him up.

I can't remember whether you've ever been to Canada. I know at Burmah it was always regarded as the equivalent of the salt mines, and you probably recall poor old Wally Forbes who was sent out to look after Montreal that time they caught him in flagrante with the Chairman's secretary during the staff outing to Ostend. Quite frankly I can't think how the Canadians stand each other. If I was left alone with that many million bores for half an hour I'd go berserk with a meat axe.

Their leader, a fluffy little antique dealer called Trousseau, whose wife very understandably took to hard drugs and ran off with a pop-singer, is absolutely wringing wet vis-a-vis the Bear, and had M frothing at the mouth from the moment he came prancing down the steps of their equivalent of Number Ten. This distaste was very clearly reciprocated, and Trousseau insisted on the Proprietor holding forth in Froggish, sniggering the while behind her back as it became clear that neither man nor beast could understand a word she was saying. Then to cap it all he paid some hooligan to give her a nasty fright when she was going walkabout. To get her own back, M had a much-publicised reception for the Leader of the Opposition, a real crasher even by Canadian standards, who could only talk about the cent by cent rise and fall in the price of paper over the last forty years. He invited us to pop up to his cabin in the Rockies for three months any time we felt like a spot of orienteering. Would you believe it?

Naturally enough I got blind drunk on touching down and stayed that way for the duration of our visit, with the result that I was very seriously ticked off for snoring during reptiles' question time!

When I tell you that it was a relief to arrive in Washington and be greeted by old Hopalong, needless to say holding hands with his tiny and emaciated spouse, you will get some idea of my feelings about the Land of the Maple Leaf.

I hadn't seen the old cowboy since his House of Lords spectacular when he came to launch his new autocue screen, and it was quite a shock. The more hair dye he puts on the weirder he looks and he can only hear if you shout into his breast pocket very loudly indeed. He put me in mind of that former Chairman of Cobbs the haberdashers in Tunbridge Wells who stayed on till he was ninety and kept being mistaken for a dummy. They used to say he had an Indian man who came round on Thursday mornings to inject powdered monkeys' balls into his bum. (You probably remember one of the window-dressers got the push for trying to get his trousers down.) I can't say for sure that Hopalong is on the same kick, but he certainly has that waxy look about the wrinkles and finds it hard to turn his head from side side.

Things in general have not been helped by the Boss's strange new Churchillian Iron Curtain mood. It all began when Van der Pump, our South African seer and backstage Rasputin, came down to Chequers one weekend and showed us his slides of the Kalahari. This was pretty ballsaching as you can imagine and I slipped away under cover of darkness to wet the whistle down at the Waggonload of Monkeys in Great Missenden. When I got back they were still sitting there, with the projector turned off and the lights on while the old sage fixed her with his hypnotic eye and spun her a yarn about some tribe of little bushmen who can bore holes in rock by looking at it. Not that this was the point of what he was saying: his burden was that these bare-arsed Johnnies are convinced that when their Big Chief turns his toes up his spirit hovers about moaning in a kind of limbo until it finds a worthy successor, at which point it moves in and everything's tickety boo. 'It's as if', he added, his eyes glowing with a mysterious fire, 'the spirit of Winston Churchill had been waiting all this time, and now at last had found its home.' I gave a nervous guffaw at this point and asked the Boss if she'd like a glass of brandy, but the other two made it clear that they found my remarks in poor taste, and it was cold tongue pie for supper that night as far as yours truly was concerned.

Anyway, the long and the short of all this is that the Boss spends hours every night in the old War Room down in the bowels of Westminster reading the Collected Speeches, and has regurgitated them all over North America whenever she has been called upon to speak. I don't know what it does to Andropov, but by God if terrifies me.

M couldn't wait to get back in order to knock hell out of Fatty Prior following the news that once again all the bogtrotters have strolled out of the so-called high security Open Prison to carry on their merry pranks. She has been looking for an excuse to bash Fatty for some time and this was absolutely heaven sent. The other little fellow waiting outside the study door with the A–D down the seat of his pants was Norman Fowler, who for some reason I still haven't fathomed is Minister of Health. All he had to do was turf out a couple of thousand nurses who will be far better off on the dole and explain to the nation why this made solid sense. Instead of which even M's lot are up in arms and there's been a great deal of talk about demolishing the Health Service. A damn good wheeze in my opinon and entre nous the Boss thinks so too. Why people put up with years on the waiting-list when they could get it all done on BUPA like Margaret and me I haven't the foggiest idea.

Blackpool looms. What say you to joining me at the Country Club as 'research staff' during the Conference? Everything on the house, very decent little course at Morecambe, and the Manager assures me there'll be no problem about licensing hours. Maurice P sounded all in favour and in cracking form – he tells me he has a brand new shrink called Mr Cleese – and the Major has promised to pencil it in as long as he can bring his new lady-friend – the one who keeps the kennels near Aldershot. I couldn't really say no; she's an absolute pain but she usually passes out fairly early on and never comes to before lunch-time. Can I count on you?

Take it easy now. Have a real nice day buddy boy and may the Good Lord take a liking to you.

DENIS

10 Downing Street
Whitehall

21 OCTOBER 1983

Dear Bill,

What a shambles! If I ever needed convincing of the virtues of alcoholism in preference to a little bit of fluff on the side, this whole sad tale of Cecil Parkinson and his love child has hammered it home good and proper. Quite honestly, Bill, I never took much of a shine to him. Altogether too much of an arse creeper as far as the Boss was concerned, and he really got my goat during the election campaign by bagging the seat next to the driver on the Bus and forcing me to sit at the back with the reptiles, all singing Roll Me Over In The Clover and tossing beer-cans out of the window at the unemployed. You or I could tell he was an HMG with his eye on the main chance, but the Boss is always far too busy to notice things like that. All she saw was the flashing smile, the Brylcreemed charm, clean-cut appearance and sober demeanour.

Of course, I knew aeons ago that our Mr P. and his typist friend were up to a bit of malarkey, though I thought it imprudent to tell you at the time. It was the Major's chum, Four-Eyes Entwhistle, who spotted them canoodling in a wine bar in Chester and inevitably put two and two together. Major on the blower next morning, wasn't it my duty to tell the Boss? I said absolutely not. Whatever I thought of our Cecil, we chaps must stick together etc. If one person starts blowing the whistle on that kind of caper where will any of us be? And in any case I deemed it probable that a messenger bearing such tidings to the Boss would have a life expectancy measurable in seconds.

Come election night on June 9th, champagne corks popping, M, self and Cecil pull in from the window after our eighth curtain call from the cheering winos in the street below, CP clears throat, 'Prime Minister, I have something to tell you. Could I perhaps speak to you privately?' Margaret, still in euphoric mood, bids him proceed, all friends here. Out comes a lot of romantic novelette drivel about how he is deeply in love with a very wonderful woman, she has taught him the true meaning of the word for the first time, would like Margaret to be the first to know that she is expecting his child, will she be the godmother? Crikey, Bill, did she hit the roof!! Talk about cruelty to animals! Had he ever considered his duty to his employer, the little woman waiting up night after night at Downing Street to hear his report on morale in the constituencies? And all the time his thoughts had been elsewhere! Parkinson stammered something about Lawson having got away with it – you probably remember Bill, his wife skedaddled with a randy egghead from Oxford and he sought solace in the arms of a lady librarian at Halitosis Hall, all pretty squalid I agree but that's the way things go. The Boss however refused to be diverted. Had he forgotten that the election had been won with the help of young Bertie Mount on the platform of The Family? Unless he pulled his trousers up pronto and got himself taken back into the bosom of Mrs P and PDQ it was curtains as far as his political career was concerned. What the hell could have got into him etc, all over again, you know the form, and I was finally moved to lay aside my

personal feelings, crack a bottle of rotgut and force it between his chattering teeth.

Time goes by, all apparently tickety boo, the whole thing swept under the carpet; this however reckoning without the reptiles or indeed Miss Keays. Hell hath no fury etc, as Picarda discovered that time he ditched the big woman from Harrods' Food Halls who subsequently came at him with the broken bottle. Come September, reptiles on the line to HQ every morning asking for a statement. Boss belatedly realising that solids are about to hit air-conditioning, gives CP heave-ho as party chairman and moves in little Bummer, who, whatever his other shortcomings could not conceivably be accused of being a part-time swordsman. I could tell that her patience was beginning to wear a trifle thin however when it all blew up again on the eve of the Blackpool Circus. Once again CP was hauled in, given the gestapo cellars treatment and ordered to come clean, tell all, and Saatchis would push the loyalty line, the Party's readiness to move with the times etc.

A sticky wicket, I think you'll agree. We arrive at Blackpool – hordes of reptiles loving every minute of it. Parky goes in to bat, all the delegates instructed to applaud. Boss already not in best of moods, the Conference as a whole being pretty grisly, Brittan, Lawson et al getting the bread roll treatment and a lot of murky little blackshirts and gay-boys crawling out of the woodwork to make it all look very seamy. This, mark you, supposed to be the Party's celebration for the greatest victory in recent history! M, however, always sanguine, is convinced she can dispel any unhappy memories with a great Churchillian speech on the Friday, annihilating the critics, blasting the wets, knocking cocky little Pillock off his perch, and above all burying the whole Parky episode as a nine-day wonder a thousand feet underground.

Picture the scene in the early hours of Friday morning. After a sleepless night in our hotel bedroom with Bertie Mount and Sir Custardface the gag writer complete with silk dressing gown and cigarette holder having beavered through the hours of darkness to get the great oration ready for the Hopalong prompting screen, the telephone jangles to inform us that Miss Keays has blown the gaff and is plastered all over the front page of the new look gutter Times. I don't think Parky will forget the moments that followed as he ruminates about what might have been on the verandah of his sheep farm in Australia.

On the whole just as well you didn't come. I think apropos my own retirement plans at Dunleadin, Lamberhurst, that I begin to espy a light at the end of the tunnel. Thank God there is a real feeling of defeat in the air at last. It has come to something when Norman Tebbit is looked upon as our Great White Hope.

Yours,

DENIS

## 10 Downing Street
## Whitehall

4 NOVEMBER 1983

Dear Bill,

Forgive me for breaking off rather abruptly in the middle of our jaw about Grenada the other night, but Margaret's temper has been getting very frayed of late. You were, I think, asking why the hell the old girl had come out strongly against Hopalong, when surely we were all a hundred per cent in favour of exterminating the Red menace wherever it shows its ugly head.

The answer, which I could hardly give to you with the Boss hovering at the back of my neck, was that she was extremely miffed at being left out of the act. Personally I couldn't quite see what all the hoo-ha was about. As you probably know it's about half the size of the Isle of Sheppey, and largely given over to the manufacture of postage stamps. Scatty Longmuir once spent a holiday there by mistake, under the impression he'd booked into the other place in Spain – a perfectly understandable error if you go to your travel agent straight after lunch. He said the only difference was that it took much longer to get there, and the local restaurant didn't serve paella. Otherwise it was just a lot of chaps sitting about in shorts drinking rum.

Be that as it may, the first wind M got of it was when the landing craft were churning up the beach. It then transpired of course that the FO wooftahs had masterminded yet another utter ballsup. God knows, Bill, after the Falklands business, you'd think they'd have cleared out some of the human refuse clogging the Office in question, but no. Telexes rerouted to some

Swedish mail-order firm in Soho, everyone convinced that lynching the Prime Minister and massacring the Cabinet are all part of the tourist drive, and in charge of this shower old Howe shuffling about in brothel creepers with his specs steamed up not understanding a blind word of what was going on.

I always said it was a mistake moving him from the Exchequer, where he was in his element, sorting through the tax returns and occasionally going on the television to assure us all that there was light at the end of the tunnel, and meanwhile would we like to invest our remaining savings in some of his new bonds at a very generous five and a half per cent before tax? Probably if you'd had a few you might even have believed him and no doubt many did. But put him on the gunboat platform on the other hand or prop him up in the House to wave the flag for Queen and Country and he cuts a pretty sorry figure. No wonder Johnny Foreigner lays in supplies of the stale bread rolls whenever he appears over the horizon.

Had little Howe or any of his pansy advisers been on the ball, M would of course have been fully briefed well in advance, and yomped in there with the Boys from Belize, scorching the arse off every Cuban in sight within a matter of minutes. Nothing she would have liked more than a bit of Cuban arse-scorching hand in hand with old Hopalong. Ever since the Falklands show in fact she's been longing to have another crack at a bit of war-war, to quote her favourite character in fiction, and it would have done wonders for the ratings.

Another blow to her carefully laid plans was little Cocky Kinnock's first day at school. According to her scenario it was to

42

be full turnout of Smellysocks and reptiles, Cocky K on his feet ranting away about the evils of the NHS Cuts – if you can be said to rant with permanent laryngitis – Boss sits there smiling, letting out the line and then wham, reels him in and clocks him over the head with a mallet. (Cue for Smellysocks to wonder if they've made the right decision. Would they have done better with Fattersley?) As things turned out the Grenada storm blew up engulfing Howe and leaving the Boss shouting away about her deep respect for Hopalong, how only the dearest of friends can hurl abuse at one another etc. Roars of laughter, catcalls and general derision from Smellysocks, M ashen-faced and eyeing Howe's jugular in a very nasty way.

What else, you ask? We all had a good laugh at Sailor Ted's amusing denial about the porno snaps. I must say the thought of our old seafaring chum grappling heroically with some portly body of indeterminate years while the Old Bill looked on notebook in hand, was an unlikely one. But people will believe anything nowadays. I met someone the other day at the Club who asked me in all earnestness whether it was true that little Gummer likes dressing up in rubberwear and being pelted with fruit salad. This always happens in my experience whenever something like the Parkinson story comes out. Do let me know if you hear anything about *me*.

Yours in leatherwear,

DENIS

 10 Downing Street
Whitehall
18 NOVEMBER 1983

Dear Bill,

I've just come back from the annual Remembrance Day Parade in Whitehall, where I was lucky enough to bump into Peg-leg Hartridge, who was marching past with his British Legion contingent from Staines. I managed to wink at him as he stumped by the saluting base, and we met up afterwards in the Guardsman's Arms, for a couple of large ones and a few guffaws about old times. He was tickled pink at the way the Boss had stopped any nonsense about that shifty little greaser Doctor O getting in on the cenotaph act and having his photograph in the papers looking statesmanlike. As Peg-leg said, the most the little Doctor had done in the service of King and Country was letting off a few blanks on Salisbury Plain during his days in the school OTC. Of course you could say exactly the same of Steel and Cocky Kinnock, but as I pointed out to Peg-leg, you can't have too many conchies cluttering up the plinth, and he absolutely agreed. Allow the Doctor on in his funeral gear and where would it end? Next thing you know there'd be Scargill on parade with a CND banner, not to mention hosts of frightful wooftahs representing the fallen gays in two world wars. You may chuckle, Bill, but that's the kind of thing we're up against nowadays.

Talking of which, I thought the Lord Chief Justice was very sound when he said they ought to bring back the rope for buggers. An unfashionable view, Bill, but it is high time somebody spoke up for the silent millions of people like you and me whose whole way of life is under attack.

Poor old Howe is still getting stick I see. You remember last year he lost his trousers on the train. We all had a good laugh at that. The latest tale relates how he poured a pot of hot coffee into his crutch in the Executive Class en route for Athens and another shouting match with our loyal comrades in Europe. I gather he had to borrow a pair from Lofty Smallhouse of the FO to avoid the spectre of walking naked into the conference chamber. Gales of merriment nevertheless from the evil-smelling foreigners as he shuffled in.

It all points again to the fact that the Boss made a major boo-boo in ever moving him from the Treasury and replacing him with our friend at Number Eleven, Mr Nicely Nicely. God, Bill, what a prat! I know that the Good Book instructs us to love our next door neighbours, but that man would try the patience of a saint. Here we are, pledged to reduce inflation to zero, rising prices the number one evil, sworn to give British industry the shot in the arm it needs to get it off the slab, and up comes Nicely Nicely authorising huge increases in the retail cost of gas and electricity. As you know from Smallbone, these sods are making massive profits as it is. All they ever do is sit around in white coats in huge humming laboratories reading the Guardian and occasionally looking at a dial or twiddling a little knob. Makes no sense to me.

44

I taxed Nicely Nicely with it the other morning when he was watering his hair in the downstairs gents prior to popping in to see the Proprietor. I was given the usual snooty brush off, and made to feel that until I got an A plus in O-level economics I shouldn't bother him with my views and might as well save my observations for my fellow winos down at the Club. Fair enough no doubt in today's abrasive society, but I was brought up to treat my seniors with more respect.

The only person who's prepared to stand up to Little Lord Fauntleroy is that old city slicker Peter Walker, the sole surviving wet in Margaret's entourage. However come High Noon in the Cabinet Room it transpired that PW had gone AWOL in China, leaving some whippersnapper of an office boy to face the bowling, with the result that Little Lord F. carried the day. I am told his head is even more swollen than it was before and I suppose I must steel myself to more instances of cheek in the corridor.

Any minute now Hopalong's missiles should be landing at Newbury, much to the dismay of the great unwashed. I must say, in view of the continuing froideur between M and the old gunslinger, I can't think it's entirely reassuring. According to Heseltine they're still clinging to the hope of a last-minute deal at Geneva with the Russkies climbing down. However Boris, who is always reliable on the Soviet scene, tells me that Andropov died in August and that they can't agree on who's to be the next Tsar. I said I thought Hopalong was probably dead as well by the looks of him, so I wouldn't have thought there was much hope of intelligent debate.

How are you finding your new clubs? I'm told the Korean ones are twice as good at half the price, but Lillywhites were out of stock so I won't know till Christmas. God, to think that's all looming up again! Still, when you get to our age I suppose you can't complain. All I notice is that the drinks seem to get weaker. Has that been your experience?

Yours as the shades lengthen,

DENIS

2 DECEMBER 1982

Dear Bill,

Would you believe it? I hunted through every backstreet in Goa and not a sign of Wino Beamish. Are you sure he said Goa and not Samoa? The person I did run into, now running a string of illegal off-licences out there was Ozzie Baverstock, who you may remember used to be in the Export Office at Atlas Preservatives until he was caught coming in on Sundays and altering the books. I always had a soft spot for him, and he's absolutely fallen on his feet in Southern India, married to a very nice local lady, several khaki offspring and a villa in the hills.

The Commonwealth Durbar itself was an absolute waste of time. HM in her element, and the only person who enjoys it, as far as I could see. Little Nyerere has only to start telling his joke about the three Scotsmen and the missionary and she's off in gales of laughter, slapping him with her handbag and begging him to stop. For the rest of us it was the usual vile-smelling conference halls, hard-arsed chairs, and interminable harangues from brother coon on the evils of imperialism. Hopalong's name taken in vain by one and all, with the exception of a few American-speaking coons from the West Indies whose belief it was that the sun shines out of his fundament by day and night and that he can do no wrong.

This inevitably made for a certain atmosphere of disagreement. Not that it makes a blind bit of difference whether they agree or not. The only point of these conferences, as you or I know from our weekend seminars in Burmah days is to shunt the buggers off to the back of beyond and keep them busy until opening time. They spent about four days trying to decide what to do about Cyprus, as if it had anything to do with them or they could do anything about it, and eventually decided to call on both sides to see fair play, set up assorted committees and report back in due course.

The real point of the exercise, as I have now finally rumbled, is that the FO wallahs, who all have boyfriends in these parts, try to fix up as many freebies to sunnier climes as possible during the winter months, and Saatchis came to the conclusion it wouldn't be a bad idea if the old girl came along as well.

46

Like you I was without my Sunday Telegraph at the weekend so have yet to catch up on the golfing. I heard on the grapevine that the Major, who had supplied the plastic beakers for the beer tent, got caught with his trousers down when the Bob Hope show folded, but there was no mention of it in the Goa Gleaner, which was full of Mother Gandhi's latest edicts on the need for condoms. M's advisers have got their knickers in a great twist about the Fleet Street chaos, though why anyone should give a damn about that shower having to shut up shop for a few days when you can get all the racing results and share prices off the local radio, unless you happen to be stuck in the Goa Gandh-o-tel (see above), beats me.

As usual no-one has the foggiest idea how it all blew up. Apparently some gallant little darkie called Eddie Shah gave a handful of yobs their cards for playing sillybuggers in the night room. The next thing you know hordes of well-heeled Trots and troublemakers arrive by charabanc, set up their braziers and begin lobbing bricks at the local constabulary. Of course M's new Tebbit regulations were all designed to bring an end to this kind of carry-on, Brother Shah merely needing to have his complaint processed through the courts and bingo gets his money back. This is reckoning without the bone-headed obstinacy of the NGA lot, who have carved out a very nice little set of sinecures for themselves and their relatives over the years and aren't over-anxious to see the arrangement brought to an end. You may remember that Sailor Ted got himself into a similar fix when he

47

tried to crack down on the dockland yobbos who were working the same kind of fiddle, nicking videos etc. Will the Boss succeed where poor old Ted failed? Margaret is in no mood to get involved, being far too busy on the current round of freebie package tours to the winter sunshine, and it's all being left to little Tom King, who has taken over Our Norman's bed of nails. A nice enough cove, but hardly the man to take a stick to these East End freeloaders.

All of that apart, Saatchis are dead keen to chalk up a mini-Falklands with the Smellysocks, so the Boss may be wheeled out against her better judgement to sound off against the printers. The ad men have been rather rattled of late by the decline in enthusiasm for our side, particularly among Margaret's so-called intellectual heavy mob. The latest defector is a marmalade-haired brown-tonguer called Paul Johnson who hit the headlines when there were headlines with a lot of boo hoo hoo stuff about M having let him down over Grenada. But as I pointed out to Gow, no-one at the Club had ever heard of him, though one man thought he might have seen him years ago on the telly in a programme about epilepsy and said he used to be a Communist. So why anyone should give a monkey's cuss what the little bugger thinks one way or the other I can't understand. The other defector in recent days is young Bertie Mount, who was in the think tank. Some dispute I gather about the length of his lunch break, and he's sloped off back to the Drones Club. Ah me, sic transit gloria Mounti.

That's it for now,
Signing off,

DENIS

48

Dear Bill,

First things first. Will you be *sure* to pick up a jumbo crate of the Gordon's duty free from Maurice's end of fire sale and deliver it *before* the 23rd, which is when we leave for Purgatory Bucks. Do for God's sake use the tradesmen's entrance, which is further down, as there have been several embarrassing episodes in the past, one of them in front of the reptiles. I think I may be able to wangle a 72-hour pass after Boxing Day, in which case we might manage a few holes at Huntercombe, weather permitting. (If wet in church hall.)

I can't make out quite what is going on at the moment up here at the sharp end. Who should I see coming out of the Boss's office the other morning but Lord Lakedistrict, Old Oystereyes as was, who we all thought had been safely tucked up in the bed nearest the door following his years of faithful service, heavy drinking etc. He was looking a bit bewildered, and readily accepted my offer of a scoop in the den, prior to elevenses. The old buffer shook his head sadly for a bit, puffing and blowing as is his wont, and asked me if I had any idea what was eating M.

Apparently, though this is obviously between ourselves, the Boss had got it into her head that her slice of the market mediawise has taken a downturn. (You'll forgive the Saatchi-speak but we all talk this way nowadays.) As the old squire readily conceded, the shine has rather gone off the apple. Ever since Parky let the team down with his bit on the side, the solids have been hitting the air-conditioning with pretty monotonous regularity. DHSS cuts, Lawson obviously out of his depth, Howe spilling porridge down his trousers all the time, Pym and the wets yapping away the moment Margaret's back is turned. All less than satisfactory. I nodded, and refilled the old boy's beaker. Then he dropped the bombshell. Who has Margaret in her wisdom appointed to stop the rot imagewise but OO, Lord LD himself. I did my best to stop my face betraying a rictus of alarm at this news, but honestly, Bill. Suppose the MCC were to decide to bring back Denis Compton, who has been hitting the optics pretty relentlessly for the last forty years, to defeat the Ozzies! You'd think that was pretty rum, wouldn't you? Old

Willie, to do him credit, is not so far gone for the thought not to have staggered across his own mind, but he was always putty in the Boss's hands, so all I could do in the circs was to offer my support and another large one for the stairs.

Since I last screwed the Basildon Bond into the Olivetti Margaret has also had a disastrous tiff with two of her boyfriends, to wit the King of the Frogs and the Old Gunslinger. You know what the French are like from the time Daphne was pestered by that wine salesman from Bordeaux and you got left with a garage full of Appellation Controlee Algerian turps. Mitterrand is very much in the same mould, always turning up with bouquets of forced roses in cellophane, a lot of kissing of hands and the usual kind of slobbering romance one associates with our friends across the Channel, and then five minutes after he's gone you notice the clock's missing. For months the Boss was trying to get them to see sense on all these mountains of unwanted comestibles which you and I are helping to pay storage on out of our hard-earned deposit accounts. Then they had a summit down at the war-damaged place in Greece and the whole thing broke up in disorder. If you ask me old Enoch, batty though he be, may be proved right again, in saying that it was all a great mistake and Heath will emerge as one of the blackest villains in British history.

M's other fancy-man, Donald Duck King of the Wrinklies, has also been getting no end of stick. Ever since he failed to ask

her along for the Grenada shindig it seems he can't do a thing right. Last week she amazed them at Halitosis Hall by leaping to her feet and bollocking the old boy for keeping his interest rates up, as if he was responsible for the monkey tricks practised by Furniss and his ilk at the NatWest; then he said he was going to sell weapons to the Argies and off she goes again, spitting tintacks and calling him every name under the sun. Perfectly sound in my view, but in that case why is little Howe sent down to the post office with a good luck telegram to the Chief Gaucho? All very baffling I think you will agree, and how poor old stumblebum Whitelaw is going to put things right when this kind of caper goes on I have no idea.

As if this wasn't enough we all got embroiled at the weekend in a silly publicity stunt about the nuclear holocaust organised by some bushy-tailed bugger from American TV. Heseltine, about whose balance of mind I am beginning to have my doubts, got inextricably entangled with the media and instead of ignoring it like any sensible person insisted on the right of reply, ringing up the Boss to tell her that he was on all channels simultaneously, and insisting that she shouldn't miss it. Come the night M got herself propped up in front of the TV with a box of Kleenex and a pretty stiff whisky, and the first bit looked to me very like Dallas but without the music, so I crawled out on all fours and hopped it down to the Waggonload of Monkeys for their Christmas happy hour and found a very good crowd of inebriates all getting into training for the Festive Season. By the time I'd located my latchkey and tiptoed in holding the brogues I assumed the whole thing would be over and the Boss would have hit the hay. Not so. From what was going on on the screen I thought it must be the News at Ten, but it was still the Nuclear Epic, M entranced until the last maimed survivor had crawled from the screen. Stand by for another attack on Hoppo for allowing this kind of sensationalism to undermine morale in the West.

I'm hoping the old girl will put her feet up a bit come Christmas: but the usual crew of deadbeats, retired middle management and actor laddies hungry for honours are due to descend for hot punch on Boxing Day. I shall think of you and Daphne in Marbella chez Mrs Hotchkiss, relict of the Wingco.

Yuletide Glee,

Yrs with a filthy hangover,

DENIS

# C H E Q U E R S

Dear Bill,

I must apologise for the black-edged communication informing you of my demise due to over-indulgence: this was one of Mark's little Yuletide jokes that as usual misfired as I may say did the Major's Singing Gorillagram on the 23rd who was summarily arrested at the gate and bundled off to choky, security having been beefed up considerably since the IRA's pre-Christmas goodwill mission at Harrods Stores. Apropos, you probably spotted me on the Nine O'Clock News doing my business-as-usual bit. At the time I was fairly browned off, having left the house en route for Lillywhites and a last minute foray into the Golf Department to collect my Japanese ball-washers for miscellaneous chummos, including yourself I may say, when up goes a window and the Boss calls me back: Saatchis have a limo waiting at the corner to ferry me down to Harrods, buy whatever I like on M's account as long as it doesn't cost more than fifteen quid, and back in time for the photo-call at half six.

I don't know when you were last in Harrods, Bill, but I still have happy memories of going there for a bit of fun in the zoo and a tickle of the ivories in the piano department before they opened at the Bunch of Grapes. Always a very nice class of person in there, and you usually ran into someone you knew in the banking hall. My God! What would poor old Potty Fergusson say if he could see the swarms of great fat begums in beaks and Allah-catchers busily shoplifting everything they can lay their dusky hands on, followed by their pathetic little sheikhs, none of them housetrained and all smelling like polecats!

I tracked down the sports department somewhere on the upper deck and asked for a dozen of the Jap ball-washers. Very sorry Sir, not much demand, temporarily out of stock, expecting consignment early in the New Year; had I thought of trying Lillywhites? I eventually left the store with a collection of assorted miniatures to hang on the tree and an Old Millhillian cricket square for Mr Wu who has always admired mine. Back at the barracks reptiles all assembled, contents of bag emptied out with much tut-tutting and headshaking by the creep from Saatchis, shunted off in the direction of the camera lights and told to say something Churchillian on the need to keep the tills rattling at Christmas tide come what may. In the event I rather lost my temper, but the Major told me it came over very well on the bulletin. Needless to say by the time I got down to Lillywhites they were shut.

By the by, do you see that furry-headed little cookie-pusher Brittan is having the fountains in Trafalgar Square drained for New Year's Eve? You might warn your friends not to make the trip this year. As I told him, revellers could easily hurt themselves very badly, jumping off the statuary in the expectation of a jolly good splash and landing flat on their backs on the concrete. As for his crack down on drink and driving, I've never heard anything so monstrous. No wonder the IRA get away scot-free when every copper in creation is lurking in the hedgerow with pencil licked eager to book the public-spirited boozer for doing everything in his power to prevent unemployment in the Highlands.

I am sorry to say I missed most of the festivities, having passed out after unwisely opening Mark's present on Christmas Eve, a bottle acquired at the duty free shop in Macau and called I think Number One Tiger Breath Whisky. The son and heir did his usual act of descending unannounced, on this occasion in the company of Mr Monty Glew, a swarthy little chancer from Finchley who he introduced as his accountant. Having plied me rather too obviously with my own very expensive gin within moments of their arrival, they broached the little matter of an interest-free non-returnable loan to help tide them over until they receive a promised order for seven gull-winged convertibles, to be sold to an influential client in Dubai. I could tell from the cut of his jib that little Mr Glew was up to every trick in the book, his eyes flickering over the furniture and fittings, no doubt with a view to how much they would fetch in the Portobello Road, and my cheque book remained firmly tucked away in the breast pocket. Mark later tried a bit of the Lawson-type flannel on M about confidence returning, leading out of the recession etc, but she also kept her handbag securely shut and later rang through to the Waggonload of Monkeys to book a single room for Mr Glew overnight.

It was after lunch that I toddled up to the den, feeling the need for a stiffener, and made the mistake of starting in on the Chinese poison in front of the Channel Four Golf Highlights of the Year. When I came to it was Boxing Day and the chirping of a lone sparrow on the windowsill went through my head like the rattle of a Bofors gun. The only mercy, as Wu explained to me on the

drive down to Hoddinott's surgery for a pick-me-up and emergency Kaolin, was that I'd missed the Howes who had come over on Christmas night, also Hopalong's personal video message not to mention Van der Pump's midnight phone call with his predictions for the coming year. Wu said it was the usual guff about some dream he'd had featuring Margaret as King Kong sitting on top of the Albert Memorial shying coconuts at David Owen.

I'm still feeling pretty fragile and taking it very gently with the intake of alcohol, rationing myself to no more than four large ones before meals.

Regards,
A happy 1984, and remember Big Mother is Watching You.

DENIS

# 10 Downing Street
# Whitehall

13 JANUARY 1984

Dear Bill,

Do thank Daphne for the bed on New Year's Eve. My memory of events after about two am is necessarily blurred. Did Maurice Picarda suddenly come into the Spread Eagle with a monkey on his shoulder? And was the Major breathalysed on the way back from Maidstone or did I dream that? I presume we all got home because I woke up in your granny annexe with Mrs Plimsoll pressing a welcome cup of Instant into my shaking hand with the news that you'd left on the morning cheapo from Gatwick. I suppose one is getting a bit long in the tooth for making whoopee on these occasions, but that's no reason to stop doing it.

Saatchis felt it necessary for the Boss to dispel any sense of doom at the coming of the New Year. I couldn't see that it was any more necessary than usual, but apparently some old Etonian dropout called Orwell made a lot of money just after the last show with a book called 1984, foreseeing a bleak scenario of Britain under a pretty tough law and order regime – some ugly mug running the show with the help of a Databank and sniffer dogs.

Contrast this, say the Saatchis, with the bright new world under the Boss, a radiantly beautiful if mature woman, with everyone free to do whatever they like so long as they can afford it, plenty of colour TV sets for all, inflation growling in its cage, altogether a boom boom boom situation.

By the by, I don't know if you saw but I thought it was a bit rich of the Saatchi Bros to launch out as television critics, and issue an in-depth bollocking to ITV for failing to come up to scratch. Obviously the Boss's patronage has gone to their heads and the next thing you know they'll be criticising the Test Team or telling the Archbish to pull his socks up. Not a bad idea incidentally, but hardly the sort of thing one wishes to hear from a couple of jumped-up Eyetie icecream pedlars.

My own contribution to getting the economy back on its feet again was to drop in on Furniss at the NatWest on the first working day after Christmas to see how my deposits were looking in the wake of the Xmas battering. He too was doing his best to dispel the Orwellian despair with a glossily produced porno-graphic calendar which he offered to me discreetly wrapped with the compliments of the management. Would I care for a beaker of his new Cyprus sherry? Our bald friend proceeded to sound a note of steady optimism waving the inside pages of the FT at me in a grandiose manner and producing graphs showing growth on its way through the ceiling. I had the usual feeling of deja vu, asked for my printouts and another slug of the Cypriot filth, and rather stopped him in his tracks with what seemed to me a logical query: if everything in garden so delightful, why he jack up mortgage rates?

Thoughtful pause, fingertips together, brow creased in cogitation, then rapidly turns conversation to holiday plans, the wife and kiddies v excited about a brochure called Tunisun etc.

Not a word to Bessie, but I detect some anxiety about the little ginger prat i/c Smellysocks. He got in some bit of Ozzie crumpet to do his PR, bought himself a new suit from M & S and lined up a lot of diplomatic freebies in order to get the usual collection of snaps, me with Hopalong, me with Mitterrand, me at Andropov's tomb etc, thus creating the erroneous impression he knows his arse from his elbow. He didn't get off to a good start when he flew off to Athens, and emboldened by a couple of stiff ouzos, started ogling that musty old Greek Bag who used to sing Never on a Sunday and is now Entertainments Officer out there. Before you could say eureka, there was Pillock swaying to and

from W Pediment of Par-
-thenon · Cephisus
BRITISH MUSEUM

fro, pledging undying devotion to the Glories that were Greece and promising to send back the Elgin Marbles as soon as he got elected. What the hell does he know about it anyway? Next thing you know we'll be giving back Cleopatra's Needle to the Indians. I mean to say, surely the whole point of the British Museum is that it should be British. It's not the Greek Museum even if it looks like it. I told the Boss to put this in one of her speeches but I don't think it sank in.

What else is new? Poor little Howe has been given his jabs, ten pairs of spare trousers and sent trundling off round the Middle East, and the Monk who we'd all assumed to be languishing in the funny farm suddenly resurfaced with a three-hour speech on the need for more 'O' level passes. Everybody seemed very impressed by this, but I think that was probably only because they thought he was in the funny farm in the first place.

You saw that Mark is taking out some rock-laden heiress in Texas. Fingers crossed we might even get shot of the little sod once and for all and see a return on our money. Who knows, I may follow in the footsteps of President Ford and get a walk-on part on Dallas: 'Here honey, meet my paw in law, the Limey Wino'.

May the Lord bless you real good.

DENIS

# 10 Downing Street
# Whitehall
27 JANUARY 1984

Dear Bill,

What a very enjoyable trip to the Land of Apartheid and Sun. Every time I go there I can't understand why everyone makes such a fuss about their local rules and regulations. Looking at the smiling faces in the street you could tell that a pretty good time was being had by one and all, and as Mrs Van der Keffersbesher said at the farewell wine and cheese, we whites have got to stick together against the reds, blacks, pinkos and everybody else. All common sense stuff, but if the Boss was to stand up and say as much on the TV the roof would fall in. Don't ask me why, it's just the mad kind of world we live in.

You probably saw on our return that the reptiles, having failed to trace us in the Transvaal, are trying to make trouble for the Proprietor over the boy Mark. I don't need to tell you the difficulties we've been through with the little bugger in the past, first of all with advertising rubber goods on the side of racing cars, then all the hoo-ha when he got himself lost with a French bint in the Sahara and had to be rescued by the combined air forces of the North African Treaty Organisation, not to mention his latest exploits flogging Japanese plonk and Hong Kong scent on behalf of some fly-by-night outfit at present being scrutinised by the Revenue.

Now the Smellysocks are trying to make trouble about him getting mixed up in cement in the Middle East. I don't know if you recall a particularly grisly tour the Boss and I undertook to Sidi Barrani and points East three years ago. I didn't tell you at the time because it seemed of no conceivable interest, but during a scheduled stopover in Oman, who should come breezing into the VIP lounge in dark glasses and a girly mag under his arm, but the son and heir. What a coincidence etc, temporarily strapped for dibs, could I bung him a few travellers' cheques, and while we were about it, could he tag along for the cocktail sausages at the Sultan's Palace as he hadn't had anything to eat since Gatwick at breakfast time?

I was pretty livid having finally cornered the Grand Vizier Abdul Abulbul and tried to do my sales pitch on behalf of poor Maurice's double-glazing caper, then, as you may recall, poised on the brink of bankruptcy, when Mark charges up, would you believe it, brushes me aside, lays an arm round the sheikhly shoulders, and draws him off into a corner making great play of family solidarity, nothing likely to please the Great White Mother more than three hundred million or so towards another close relative called Cementation Limited knocking them up a little polytechnic on a suitable site overlooking the harbour. Interested nods from friend Snaggleteeth, new gleam in the eye, and thumbs down from a menial on Maurice's double-glazing.

Be that as it may I thought nothing more until it all floated to the surface again last week, questions asked in the House, Margaret being 'got at' through Mark, as if either of us were in any way responsible for the little twerp at his age. I told her to get up at Halitosis Hall and say as much, but Saatchis advised a no comment approach, Margaret's bloke i/c reptiles to complain to lobby about unfairness etc, which means that it will fester away for months with yours truly getting regular bollockings from the Boss into the bargain, and all murky business contacts, to wit you, Maurice and the Major constantly under surveillance.

What with one thing and another M has had a pretty trying time. She was all set to get a new war going on the Red Barons at County Hall, who as you probably know are always shovelling public money into the handbags of every conceivable variety of queer and weirdo – a long overdue campaign that had the full backing of Saatchis and was scheduled to rocket her back into the charts like greased lightning. Instead of which the wets decide to protest against what they term interference with local democracy, the resulting uproar awakens Captain Ted in his hammock a-sleeping there below, and he comes rumbling out to put the boot in to roars of helpless mirth from the Smellysocks. What the blue-rinsed hero always fails to realise is that his little interventions nearly always succeed in letting the Boss off the hook.

Not to be outdone, old Brer Enoch, weary of sniping at the Boss, decides to go one higher and take a pot shot at the Monarch, accusing her of pandering to the darkies in her Christmas TV show. Admittedly I was pretty far gone on Christmas afternoon, but it did strike me at the time as a bit odd that instead of sitting at her desk, surrounded by signed photographs of the Russian Royal Family in silver frames and a few nice chrysanths, she chose to address us from a camp stool on the lawn at Gandhi Towers. I assumed it was all to do with everything on the telly being about India nowadays, but what Enoch doesn't understand, bless his little cotton socks, poor barmy bugger, is that HM eats, dreams and sleeps all that Commonwealth nonsense, and her idea of bliss is being smothered in garlands and carried through the bush shoulder high by half-naked coons while a lot of little missionary-trained pygmy Johnnies throw their spears in the air and sing God Save the Queen. You don't get the same feeling riding down the Mall in a taxi on a wet Friday afternoon.

Yours restored,

DENIS

# 10 Downing Street
# Whitehall

Dear Bill,

I did enjoy our celebration of the Chinese New Year during the Boss's absence in the Land of the Magyars. As I think I may have explained to you later on in the evening, I put my foot down pretty firmly on the idea of tagging along on that particular jaunt. I once had to share a sleeper with a Hungarian publisher on the Flying Scotsman who spent the whole night lying in his underpants on the top bunk smoking cigars and telling me disgusting stories about his relations. When he finally fell asleep just north of Watford he began to snore in a strong Hungarian accent rattling the very ironwork, and I determined then and there never to have any more truck with the Buda pests. (My little joke.)

As it turned out, following the rumpus over Mark, the Boss was keen to be seen out solo for fear the reptiles might accuse me or the boy of trying to wangle another contract out of the Commies. Some hope. According to Maurice's uncle Siggy who was in pre-cast chicken coops before he was put away, they rob you blind as soon as you step off the plane and even then you need a letter of introduction from Harold Wilson and a few fifty quid notes folded into your passport.

Apropos the family blister, Kinnock and his malodorous crew are still trying their damndest to make things hot for all of us over the Oman caper. Shore, the dissipated-looking one with the pot belly and the hair falling over his eyes, got up off his hunkers last week and accused the Boss of being some latter-day Al Capone, urging her to make a clean breast of it and seek sanctuary in Holloway. Meanwhile the reptiles are trying to make something out of my efforts on behalf of Maurice's double-glazing enterprise to suggest that I was up to my neck in the cement deal. Anyone could have told them that double-glazing was a very tricky putt to sink with the temperature well over a hundred and ten degrees. I remember telling Maurice so at the time, pointing out on my return that what buildings there are don't even have windows. True, I may have put in a word, once Mark had sewn up his university deal, on behalf of that friend of the Major's who does sauna units and barbecues, but I'm sure nobody could possibly have heard about that and I was assured there was nothing on paper.

Most of the flak, thank God, has been diverted to poor Brother Howe, the little Welsh cove who keeps losing his trousers. As I may have said before, he was perfectly satisfactory cooking the books round at the Treasury and going on TV once a year to explain why fags were going up another fivepence, but let him loose in the international arena and disaster ensues as surely as night follows day. I mean, quite honestly, if you were a Frog or a Krautkopf sitting in one of their high-tec air-conditioned conference halls nineteen floors up, would you jump to attention if Mogadon Man came padding along in his brothel creepers adjusting his spectacles with one hand and clutching his trousers with the other?

The latest fiasco concerns a lot of grey boffins no-one had ever heard of who are paid to sit in Cheltenham listening to Radio Moscow twenty-four hours a day and let us know what's going on over there in the way of Light Entertainment. A total waste of time if you ask me, but the Yanks attach great importance to it, as they can't get Radio Moscow in New York. Anyway, couple of weeks ago, little Howe twiddling his thumbs at the FO ups and decides that these boffins can't be allowed to play sillybuggers whenever they feel like it and if they don't agree to do things by the book they'll all get the sack.

Perfectly sensible thinking, and in anyone else's hands it would all have gone through like a dose of salts. Instead of which the whole country is now up in arms. Put me very much in mind of the frightful cock-up at Burmah you may remember when that daft bloody personnel officer Prosser-Cluff took it into his head overnight to ban smutty calendars in the Works Canteen, thus provoking a mass walkout in the Heavy Engineering Division which lost us about two million in as many days. Where is he now? You may well ask. Last I heard he was on an oil rig somewhere off Peterhead making the tea for the divers.

However there's no telling that kind of people. No earthly idea how to do anything, and the word is that when Hailsham finally hops it for the funny farm, Brer Howe will be catapulted away onto the woolsack where he can't do any further damage.

Did you by any chance see Thumper Binsley holding forth on Panorama as one of the Evil Men of the Extreme Right? He seemed to me to be making very good sense, and his views on

Whitelaw et al were sound as a bell. But it was probably ill-advised of him to wear his swastika armband, which may have given those who didn't know him the wrong impression. I personally couldn't see what all the fuss was about. Just the usual bunch of BBC pinkos trying to stir it up at your expense and mine. Next thing you know they'll be doing a hatchet job on Mark.

I tried to suggest to him the other day that he might volunteer to be the first Briton in space, but I got the impression he thought it sounded too much like hard work.

Yours fraternally,

DENIS

# 10 Downing Street
# Whitehall

24 FEBRUARY 1984

Dear Bill,

Forgive me if I was a little short on the phone last weekend but life has been a regular whirlwind of social engagements, all of which have taken their toll of my fast-dwindling reserves.

Do you remember the old boy who used to have M's job and went to Moscow in a fur hat? The story goes that his medic gave him two weeks in 1963, so he threw in the sponge, retired to the country, summoned his family for the deathbed number, only to discover shortly afterwards that he was a hundred per cent fit and well, no more than the old gents' traditional waterworks trouble playing him up. Since then he's been sitting in the pavilion making sour remarks about his successors. Anyway, having turned down the various shoddy offers put his way by Heath, Wilson etcetera to keep him quiet, he apparently read in the Telegraph that M had brought back Hereditaries for Whitelaw, whereupon he rang up and said now he'd reached the age of ninety could he have one too. Sod all that Margaret could do, I think you will agree, but put a brave face on it and cough up.

I presumed that the Proprietor could send it him through the post, but no. Saatchis in their wisdom decided that the occasion was to be marked by a champagne reception at the old buffer's country retreat down in Sussex on the way to Tunbridge Wells. So off we flocked. The old bird has always had a rather warped sense of humour and it came as no surprise as we were enjoying our pre-lunch thimblefuls of Cyprus sherry, when a powder-blue Rolls drew up and Ted Heath got out, carrying a huge bouquet of chrysanthemums and a box of cigars. The geriatric jokesmith who had clearly planned the whole thing in order to create the maximum embarrassment, then introduced Heath to M with a gracious wave of the hand murmuring, 'I don't know if you two know each other. I'm sure you have a lot in common.' Our seafaring friend coloured up to the roots at this, eliciting a snigger from the other guest of honour, the frail but sprightly Sir Alec Douglas-Home, looking very fetching in an old but carefully darned kilt.

A disgusting lunch was then served by an elderly domestic, all present preserving a frigid silence while the newly ennobled Earl rambled on about the Boss as though she wasn't there, referring to her as 'this woman with the ghastly voice who's put everyone out of work', and how in the Thirties it wouldn't have been allowed. The only good word he had to say for her was that she wasn't as bad as 'that awful organist fellow she took over from.' I could see old Deathshead Home smirking into his watercress salad at all this, and was delighted when the Ancient of Days suddenly transfixed him with a watery eye and asked whether anyone had ever told him that he bore a remarkable resemblance to that absolute ninny Alec Douglas-Home who in his opinion had started all the rot, adding that the worst thing he had ever done in his life was to hand over the reins to such a prize idiot.

Lunch broke up fairly early, and on the way back in the car M said, charitably I thought, what a terrible thing senility was, especially when exacerbated by over-indulgence. I could have told her that in my view the old walrus was as clear as a bell and was even now shaking at his fireside in helpless mirth.

As if this was not enough there has been the grisly saga of the boy Mark. Having been told to keep his mouth shut about the Oman shindig on pain of death, the little prat was then splashed all over the front pages as having given a press conference in America, offering his version of events and pledging allegiance to Margaret, the Almighty and himself. (No mention of yours truly, needless to say.) Anyway, next thing I know I am summoned into

the Proprietorial presence, expecting pretty severe flak on my involvement in Maurice P's double-glazing or the sauna units and barbecues business. You could have knocked me down with a feather when she announced that the reptiles were to be summoned to meet the son and heir at Chequers the following weekend, plus bint, in the shape of Miss Amy-Lou Fortnox, hospitality care of yours truly, church parade attendance obligatory, smiles all round and no drinking in public.

I smelt a rat at once, and was still recovering from the shock over a treble plum vodka in the pantry when Boris spelt out the plan. Saatchis have got the wind up and very understandably vis-a-vis Master Mark. After burning a good deal of midnight oil devising various schemes to neutralise him as a political threat, they hit on the weekend party as the first step towards a Not The Royal Wedding scenario, the announcement of an engagement to be made within the week, full dress ceremony at St Margaret's Westminster, where else, our hero, his Oman exploits long since forgotten, disappears shortly afterwards into the sunset equipped with a gold meal ticket for life.

All very well on paper, of course, but reckoning without the bone-headed stupidity and almost supernatural ability to foul up even the simplest of tasks that has been characteristic of the boy Mark since infancy. For further news, watch this space.

So long,
Your old granpappy,

DENIS

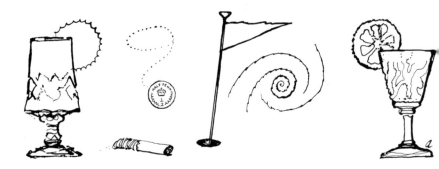

10 Downing Street
Whitehall

9 MARCH 1984

Dear Bill,

Dunleadin here we come! As you will have seen, it does now look as if things are going badly for our lot. For the first time since he came in the ginger bloke with the bandy legs i/c Smellysocks has gone ahead in the polls and our poor little wimp at Chesterfield got his arse well and truly scorched by the electors, limping in only just ahead of the Raving Monster Down With Motorways candidate.

Chaps here at HQ did a bit of whistling in the dark after the result was announced, suggesting that Benn's return to Halitosis Hall spells trouble for little Pillock. I'm afraid there may be something in this: as well as being TT I understand our friend with the revolving eyes is now a fully paid-up member of the nut-cutlet brigade and eschews all meat. You remember what happened to Maurice during his brief period on the waggon when he took up with the lady from the health food shop in Deal. His behaviour was described by the magistrate when they found him jogging up Middle Street totally starkers as 'better suited to the monkeyhouse than a quiet residential area of a leading south coast resort.' According to Doctor O'Gooley the body needs a regular intake of mutton chops to stabilise its natural rhythms, and total abstention from the amber fluid combined with a sudden intake of nuts does funny things to the brain. So Pillock had better stand by for explosions.

Talking of explosions, I have had my fair share up here at the sharp end during the last few days. After the poll came out I happened to mooch into the blue drawing-room in search of a packet of Senior Service and found M deep in Monday's copy of the Daily Telegraph. A jocular reference to our retirement plans possibly being moved forward brought the barrier of newsprint down with a sharp rustle. 'I expect treachery from Edward Du Cann, not from you!'

Mystified by this reference to the slippery little Somerset card-sharper aforesaid, I made the mistake of lingering. 'What you fail to grasp, you and your pin-striped friends up and down Whitehall, is that there has been no error of judgement over

GCHQ. I have singlehandedly taken on the combined power of the unions and the civil service and emerged triumphant. Don't interrupt, and if you must smoke do it out of the window. The workers at Cheltenham have rallied to the standard that I have raised. They have seen the light. Where is the defeat in that? Answer me!'

Knowing the form on these occasions I realised that it was pointless to argue the toss. 'Quite so,' I said, 'Quite so. I had not looked at it that way before. I am sure you are right.' 'Of course I'm right. And what is all this nonsense about me being autocratic and not listening to other people's views? When have you, Denis, found me intractable or unwilling to listen? Answer me this minute! When?' Stifling the thought that had I been so minded I could have cited instances galore of times when the spirit of give and take had been noticeably absent, I cleared my throat and inclined my head in deference to her views. 'And don't cough! Another consequence of your disgusting habit. And while we are on the subject was it you who mutilated yesterday's copy of the Sunday Times?'

I had hoped that at this point Act One Scene Two was about to be brought to an end by my rapid exit stage right, however the reference to the gaping hole on the front of the Sunday paper prolonged the agony. You probably saw it, Bill, or some friendly soul will have drawn it to your attention: further smears attempting to implicate me in the boy Mark's 'business dealings.' I myself found the whole story entirely baffling. All it amounted to, as far as I could discern, was that some snivelling reptile had rung up the boy's bank, talked to a clerk just after he got back from lunch, and elicited the fact that the boy's account was (a) overdrawn, and (b) guaranteed by yours truly. If this is the case I certainly have no memory of it. I do remember Mark turning up at Christmas time in the company of a small-time spiv called Mr Monty Glew. I am not denying that we had a few, and it may well be, Your Honour, that carried away by the Season of Goodwill, I allowed my hand to be guided across the page to affix some approximation of my signature.

Anyway, when this was all plastered across the front page of the rag in question, I deemed it prudent to cut it out, on the pretext that I was interested in a golfing report on the other side, rather than endure another helping of cold tongue pie at the breakfast table. I now got it however with knobs on and eventually retired hurt to Boris's pantry for an emergency transfusion of damson vodka. Boris in gleeful mood told me that the Kremlin were cock a hoop about the Cheltenham affair, as with everyone now predisposed to give Margaret two fingers their job of recruitment would be a great deal easier. I considered whether it was my patriotic duty to report this, but decided not.

I'll try to corner little Lawson some time this week to get you the gen on the Budget. My tip at this moment would be to turn off the electricity and stock up on the vital necessities of life. Talking of which, could you see if your friend at the Cash and Carry would deliver as far afield as Lamberhurst as measures at this end have been tightened up following the recent excitements.

Toodleoo,

DENIS

69

23 MARCH 1984

Dear Bill,

The longer I live, the more mysterious I find this whole business. Take the case of Fatty Lawson, our pomaded friend next door. We were all agreed until a day or so ago that whatever abilities he might have shown as a share tipster and mortgage-wangler in days of yore, as Chancellor of Her Majesty's Exchequer the fellow was a total non-starter even in comparison with his predecessor, the sleepwalker in hush-puppies, whose budget speeches reduced the back benchers to a snoring heap on both sides of the House.

Then suddenly, last Tuesday or whenever it was, Fatty throws off his crumpled three-piece gents' natty suiting and Shazam we are confronted with Supernigel, master of the whirling figures, saviour of the universe, number one in line to step into the Boss's shoes should the Number Eleven bus snip through the web of destiny. Damn me if I can see why.

As is my wont on these occasions, I poled down to the NatWest on the morning after to assess the damage, and found Furniss poring over his Telegraph, calculator in hand and sherry at the elbow. After a good deal of scribbling in the margin of the financial page he announced that a man in my position, ie retired executive, working wife, one wastrel son, one other female dependent, could expect to be 33p a month better off, but added with a disrespectful smirk that he didn't expect that in my own case, any small gains on such swings would compensate for losses on certain other roundabouts.

All of which makes the metamorphosis of Mr Nicely Nicely even more difficult to comprehend. I bumped into him the other evening, while I was putting the car away and it was pretty clear to me that the ecstatic notices he had received from the financial reptiles had gone to his head, already swollen in my view as it was. 'Ah Denis!' he cried with a boyish grin, flicking caviar off his waistcoat, 'Been filling up, have we? I would have thought that you and Mark could have got a tanker sent up from one of your chums in the Gulf! Ha ha ha etc.' I thought it best to still him with a chilling look, rather than retaliate by referring to the Major's experience when he invested in John Bloom's washing

machine shares as a result of matey's own spiv-like recommendations in the Telegraph some years ago.

Incidentally, as far as this Oman business is concerned, I am rather pinning our hopes on Sailor Ted coming to the rescue as so often in the past. Just as things were beginning to look a whit dodgy with all the Smellysocks queuing up to sign a chain letter deploring the existence of the boy Mark, up jumps the Broadstairs maestro, jowls awobble, to say it was high time Margaret came clean, rinsed through her smalls in public, and let him have his job back. Margaret's lobby-fodder immediately rally to the flag, put down several motions to the effect that nothing can be more admirable than a mother defending her brood however misshapen and demanding the chick in question may be.

What with the approach of Spring and the bird man of Number Eleven, spirits here have taken a depressing turn for the better, and all the talk of banana skins is now behind us. To add to the euphoria Comrade Scargill is deemed to be playing into our hands by ordering his yobbos into the fight, grinding the faces of the honest miners while old MacGregor sits on his pile of coal chuckling away and plotting his next move in the big run-down. For my part I can't wait till he's slammed down the lid on the last of the black holes, then the old boy can get to grips with ripping up the railway lines and other equally outmoded vestiges of the past.

Talking of voluntary redundancies, I understand the Monk is thinking of becoming a live-in patient rather than constantly popping out on parole as at present. I could never understand M's admiration for the crinkly-haired bean. Perfectly pleasant in his way, but daft as a brush and wholly unsuited to the rough and tumble of politics. No sign of Hailsham taking the shilling as yet. There's another one who doesn't know where he is half the time, poor old geezer.

M as you may have seen is doing her Reichenbach Falls number with the dreaded Mitterrand, of which more in my next.

Tell Daphne that if she wants to see Starlight Express she's wasting her time ringing up Gowrie. Several freebies came through the letterbox earlier this week, and I'll see to it that she gets a dozen for her bridge ladies.

Auf wiedersehen, Pat, as the German said when he pushed the Irishman over the cliff.

DENIS

6 APRIL 1984

Dear Bill,

Do you remember that story about Fruity Podmore's uncle Sidney, the so-called black sheep of the family? As I recall he was commissioned in the Royal Somerset Dragoons, lost a packet gambling, got caught red-handed with the wife of a brother officer, fiddled the Mess accounts, collapsed after taking drink at the Queen's Birthday Parade, and his father old Lord Whatsisname gave him a one-way ticket to New South Wales. As far as I know he was never heard of again.

I could not help but be reminded of this chain of events when out of the blue I got the summons to Headquarters ten or eleven days ago just after returning from a longish lunch at the RAC with Maurice and his car-dealer friend Charlie Whackett. The Boss seemed unusually fraught, and was poring over a consumer research portfolio from Saatchis marked For Your Eyes Only. 'This is all your fault Denis' was her opening salvo, 'you and your fly-by-night business friends.' For one terrible moment I thought the press must have got on to our greenhouse scheme and the little dispute with the VAT office and was steadying myself for the blow when she came at me from an entirely different direction. 'Poor Mark! If ever a promising young life was ruined by his father's total failure to give him a decent start!'

Perhaps if it hadn't been for the generous quantities of stickies ladled out by friend Whackett at the Club I might have held my peace; however on the topic of the Boy Mark I have a pretty short fuse even when sober. I therefore waded in. Had I not paid thousands in hard-earned cash to put the little sod through Harrow when Mill Hill had been good enough for me? Had I not paid for his junior membership of one of the best golf clubs in North London, indeed the one that wouldn't have Maurice? Had I not bought the little bugger the best set of children's clubs available in Lillywhite's sale, only to see him make a bonfire of them?

Self-justification, as at all times, proved unwise. 'Like father, like son' she kept on repeating, and the moment she saw my Dutch courage begin to falter, inserted her blade and began the familiar twisting process. 'Listen to me, Denis. I have done my best to cover up for the pair of you, at risk to my own survival, but now I have had enough. It is clear that the forces of disorder are not going to allow the Oman matter to drop. You got us into this mess, you can get us out of it. See the boy on neutral territory and tell him that I have arranged for him to give this interview to the Mail on Sunday. In it, as you will see, he admits amid sobs that he has brought disgrace on himself and his family, and is determined to live out his days in a far-off land in an effort to make amends.'

To say that a great weight fell from my shoulders at this moment and that I was inwardly moved to skip with glee would be no exaggeration. 'It will be hard for you', she continued, 'to break the news to our poor boy, but I am sure you have ways and means of fortifying yourself for such a daunting ordeal.' I did my best to look concerned and worried at the severity of her sentence. 'According to M15 you have just been having lunch with a man called Whackett who has connections in the motor trade in America. As a loyal citizen it is his duty to fix the boy up with some kind of sinecure. And now get out!'

I couldn't wait, and immediately gave the boy the news over the blower from the front hall, recalling the episode of the burnt golfclubs and many other milestones on the downward path, arranging for a motorbike messenger to take the interview to him for signature, and assuring him that I would put the contents of his room in Downing Street in the hands of the local refuse collectors.

All this has left the Boss ravenous for blood vis-a-vis the reptiles. Orders have gone out to Havers, the rather beaky old lawyer bird you and I ran into in the strip club during the train strike, to prosecute with the utmost rigour of the law any newspaper thought to have been in receipt of a leak, stolen memo etc, and especially the Observer who started the whole Oman snowball rolling. Rather childish in my view. Whatever your private thoughts about these ghastly vermin I always believe, with the D of E, that it's prudent to put on a cheery smile and say 'Good morning, gentlemen' when one actually meets them. Once their backs are turned of course it's another matter. Margarget however will have none of this, and was cock a hoop when one of Heseltine's typists got carried off to choky for talking to the Guardian.

How goes the revolution, meanwhile? King Arthur has been poncing about in the High Court doing his Rumpole number on investment portfolios, so attendance at the barricades has been largely kept up to strength by the various police forces bent on overtime. I don't see why they don't lock up all the pickets in a concentration camp and have done with it, as they are quite entitled to under the Tebbit legislation. Brittan, as I always suspected, is an utter ditherer, and deep down a frightful wet, so they'll just sit around waiting for the sun to come out in the hope that the only casualties will be a few OAPs who haven't had the good sense to install oil-fired central heating.

I've got some very tempting literature from the bucket shop about Easter. What do you want to do? Return to the bosom of Mother Flack on the Algarve or try pastures new? I've no idea where Lanzarote is: it looks pretty bleak from the brochure but there's rather a nice photograph of the bar. Give me a bell next time Daphne's out to lunch. Did you forget Mother's Day like I did?

Yours in disgrace,

DENIS

# 10 Downing Street
# Whitehall
20 APRIL 1984

Dear Bill,

As you may have seen in the Daily Telegraph, the Boss has zoomed off to Portugal on one of her Common Market freebies. I had been hoping to get in on the act and snatch a few days tapping the little ball across the green before relaxing beside the pool at Mother Flack's thatched oasis, but the advisors have become very sensitive about the presence on the Algarve of my alleged former business associates who might emerge from the bunkers and be photographed by lurking reptiles eager to promote another Oman shindig. I pointed out that such a scenario was highly improbable to say the least, and that any resemblance between the Sheikh of Oman and Maurice's old accountant Les Whipple, now struggling to earn an honest living packing Japanese cigars for the Canadian market was pretty remote. Anyway no joy.

Talking of wogs, I got a pretty stony look when I offered the Sheikh of Bahrain some shares in the Major's new video company. I thought I might at least try and extract something of value from two hours of dry torture at the Dorchester, but it was not to be. Incidentally, the Queen Mother gave me a very good tip about how to get through on these Mohammedan junkets last time we were staying at Balmoral. Apparently she has little miniatures concealed in specially made pockets inside her ball-gown and nips into the ladies every quarter of an hour or so for a quick slug. You and I would obviously be at a disadvantage not wearing ball-gowns but perhaps that ingenious little Mr Rothschild of yours over in Deal could run us up something in the way of evening wear with spare room under the centre vent.

Meanwhile we're all shaping up for a showdown with Scargill, the main aim being to get our own back after the defeat of '74 and to show Heath, who has been up to his usual monkeytricks at Halitosis Hall, how it should be done. I personally hae me doots as to whether Margaret's American geriatric has got the necessary will to win: he strikes me as being altogether too reasonable by half, and at his age I can't believe he packs the killer punch in the back of the neck necessary to flatten the Barnsley Bruiser. The kind of person we need in my view is someone like Prosser-Cluff in his heyday. I think when you knew him he had rather gone to seed and taken to flicking butter at the ceiling during boardroom lunches, but in his youth he was a terror. When he was in charge of our Singapore operation he single-handedly quelled a coolies' strike by locking up the ringleaders, bulldozing the native quarters, and cutting wages by fifty per cent. The funny thing was they loved him for it.

Mind you, I think the Boss has got something of a P-C about her, which is more than you can say for that pathetic squirt Tebbit or Leon the furry-headed cookie pusher who totally bungled the Bring Back Hanging Campaign. Given several months' supply of coal which no-one can afford to buy anyway, her idea is to keep a lowish profile, busy herself with trips to Portugal etc, and starve the buggers into submission, Scargill then to be led in chains through the City of London. A noble aim, I think you will agree.

Did you see the old girl doing battle on Panorama? I thought she won hands down, didn't you? The wretched Day was on the ropes from the moment the bell went and by the end so groggy he could barely stand up. I don't want to blow my own trumpet, but

I like to think I played some small part in managing the contest. As usual they arrived at Number Ten some time before the show was due to start, and while Margaret was having her nose powdered and the various gorillas were rigging up the lights, I took Brother Day upstairs to show him my golfing trophies in which he unwisely expressed an interest. Once ensconced in the leather armchair and embarked on a non-stop stream of reminiscence – how he pushed Jeremy Thorpe in the river at Oxford, how he outwitted Harold Wilson, how he could be Prime Minister by now if he could have afforded the cut in salary and so forth – he was so busy crowing away that he failed to notice that the tumbler in his right hand which I constantly refilled, laughing and nodding the while, contained a pretty powerful mixture of neat gin and Boris's Moscow Knockout Drops. When the floor manager chappie came up to collect him it took him all of three minutes to find the door, so no wonder Daphne thought he looked a bit sleepy and seemed to find it quite hard to read his own notes.

A propos Daphne's ban on our Lanzarote plans, what are you doing on Easter Monday? The Battle of Britain contingent at Huntercombe are having a Celebrity March to raise funds to pay for our Rugby Tour of South Africa, so if I come it'll have to be the dark glasses and the beard as my recent trip to the Land of the Rand went down like a lead balloon with the Great White Chief.

Happy Easter,
Yours aye,

DENIS

PS Do you agree with Maurice Picarda that if you hear Scargill's voice on the wireless in the next room he sounds exactly like Adolf Hitler?

10 Downing Street
Whitehall

4 MAY 1984

Dear Bill,
I don't think we've spoken since the ghastly business in St James's Square. As you know the Boss had toddled off to patronise the Portuguese on one of her EEC freebies, so I took the opportunity of fitting in a long delayed lunch with Thumper Binsley, last seen doing his stuff on the Panorama programme about the Nazi resurgence on the Right of the party, which little Gummer got so upset over. As I said at the time I couldn't see what the fuss was about. Thumper made a number of very sound points which were in no way invalidated in my view by his insistence on wearing a swastika armband. But a lot of people apparently didn't see the joke.

Thumper's suggestion was that we should meet for a jar or twain at the East India and Sports in St James's Square, where he is a country member, and then proceed in a leisurely manner to the RAC. Accordingly I arranged a fitting at Gieves and Hawkes for my new golfing blazer with the special Queen

Mother-style hipflask-gusset for Arab functions, and emerged into Piccadilly as Fortnum's clock was striking twelve. Cross into Jermyn Street, and blow me, the whole place is cordoned off, sheets of blue plastic hung on everything, hordes of Old Bill swarming all over the place with shooters, reptiles thick on the ground and scant respect being shown for Joe Public going about his lawful occasions.

I had asked to speak to Sir Kenneth Newman, pointing out who I was and emphasising that I had important business in the Square, when I caught sight of Thumper, as usual pretty red in the face, umbrella raised in anger and clearly about to be taken away by the guardians of the law. I succeeded in intervening, and drew him still speechless with indignation into the snug bar of the Red Lion, where the effects of two large sharpeners soon restored a semblance of equilibrium. When he finally stammered out his tale of a crazed gang of trigger-happy wogs firing machine guns through the window at all and sundry in broad daylight, I must say I could quite see why his first instinct had been to get in there and sort them out, if necessary with the end of his umbrella. After all he did spend some very colourful years in the Trucial States, and has had considerable experience with the various Mad Mullahs and bhang-befuddled bedouins who frequent those parts. As Thumper said, the only language they understand is the big stick wielded repeatedly and without mercy by the white Sahib.

Discussing these and related topics we sauntered down to the RAC where we took on board a few steadying schooners of one thing and another, toyed with the cold game pie, as usual fairly revolting, and returned to Downing Street by cab, bent on taking matters into our own hands. Thumper's scheme which seemed to me wholly sound, was to get on to his friend Hooper-Strangeways of the SAS, line up a re-run of the Prince's Gate show, and then, as soon as they were poised to blow their way in, ring up the Boss for her official go-ahead. Judge of our despair to find, squatting on the floor of the Cabinet Room talking on the telephone to Portugal with one finger in his ear, who but the smarmy little cookie-pusher Master Britoil, hush-hushing us and giving Margaret, who was obviously on our side, a lot of flannel about diplomatic protocol and the danger of retaliation in Tripoli.

I used to think Old Oystereyes was fairly pathetic, but at least he'd been in the army and knew one end of a gun from the other, whereas this fellow has spent his entire life sitting in a padded chair in the Temple counting money and musing on ways and means of screwing the next unfortunate litigant out of his precious savings. The result, as you probably saw, was humiliation. After a week of police snipers lying about on the rooftops sunbathing they decided that the whole thing was a waste of time and let the murderous little darkies trickle off home on a scheduled flight with their guns safely tucked up in the Diplomatic Bag.

I can't help feeling it would have been different four or five years ago, and I am beginning to agree with Thumper that the old girl may be losing something of her touch. Though to be fair to her, as the Major said on the phone the other night, some of our people have got an awful lot of money tied up out there. You remember that friend of Maurice's with the one arm called Macsomethingorother who's building a chain of motels in the desert. I suppose a lot of his shareholders would feel rather let down if the whole deal fell through. This chum of Maurice's, Captain Hook as they call him in the mess, is apparently a close friend of Gaddaffy, and says he's a very good sort once you get to know him. He's done a lot for the wog in the street, building hospitals and so forth with the help of our people, and holds very reasonable views on law and order at home. As I said to little Britoil after it was all over, Margaret could well take a leaf out of his book. So perhaps we did the right thing after all.

Talking of madmen, it looks as if old Scargill is beginning to sweat a bit. They're so thick these buggers they didn't realise the sun was going to come out and nobody would want their coal even if they gave it away. And I wouldn't advise Scargill to book a table at the Ritz on the strength of a whip-round by Benn. Not that I wouldn't put it past MacGregor to run up the white flag at the last minute.

Would Daphne like a test drive in this new Leyland bone-shaker? Tebbit said he could fix it, 'any time Squire', but I told him personally I wouldn't be seen dead in the thing. I'm damned if I'm going to be made a fool of by some Jap computer telling me what to do from the dashboard.

Cheeribye,
Yrs,

DENIS